DREAM HOTELS

DREAM HOTELS

Janelle McCulloch

images

Publishing

Published in Australia in 2009 by
The Images Publishing Group Pty Ltd
ABN 89 059 734 431
6 Bastow Place, Mulgrave, Victoria 3170, Australia
Tel: +61 3 9561 5544 Fax: +61 3 9561 4860
books@imagespublishing.com
www.imagespublishing.com

Copyright © The Images Publishing Group Pty Ltd 2008
The Images Publishing Group Reference Number: 823

National Library of Australia Cataloguing-in-Publication entry:

Author: McCulloch, Janelle.

Title: Dream hotels USA and the Bahamas: architectural hideaways
                    Janelle McCulloch.

ISBN: 978 1 86470 320 7 (hbk.)

Notes: Includes index.

Subjects: Hotels – United States – Design and construction.
                    Hotels – Bahamas – Design and construction.
                    Hotels – United States – Pictorial works.
                    Hotels – Bahamas – Pictorial works.
                    Architecture, Modern – United States.
                    Architecture, Modern – Bahamas.

Dewey Number: 728.5

Coordinating editor: Andrew Hall

Designed by The Graphic Image Studio Pty Ltd, Mulgrave, Australia
www.tgis.com.au

Digital production by Universal Colour Scanning Ltd., Hong Kong
Printed on 150gsm HannoArt Silk Matt, by Paramount Printing Company Limited Hong Kong

IMAGES has included on its website a page for special notices in relation to this and our other publications. Please visit www.imagespublishing.com.

CONTENTS

IN SEARCH OF THE RED, WHITE, AND BLUE

There are few places so defined by its hotels as the USA. Other destinations such as Italy, London, or Marrakech may conceive spectacularly innovative hotels and hideaways where the glamour factor is as high as the champagne glasses, but America takes hotel design to a new level. It's a truth that Americans have long understood—anything goes here.

This penchant for putting extraordinary architecture into spectacular settings has been around for the better part of a century, but it's only been in the last decade or so that Americans have really raised the stakes in the international hotel game. This is due, in part, to people like Ian Schrager, André Balazs, Kelly Wearstler, and Philippe Starck, of course; designers and hoteliers who seem to have an innate understanding of what makes for a great escape. But it's also due to an increasingly savvy generation of travelers and their awareness of aesthetics and the part design plays in creating a sense of space and place. With so many hotels opening up on the American landscape, and so many people traveling for work and pleasure now, regular (and even not-so-regular) guests are growing jaded of the same sights: the same kinds of architecture, the same kinds of interiors, the same kinds of so-called "luxury features." The travel congnoscenti don't get excited about standard luxuries such as wi-fi, power-showers, perfectly formed infinity pools, high-thread-count bed linens, flat-screen TVs, airfreight copies of cool magazines, and mini bars stocked with all sorts of premium alcohol any longer. They need more. They need hotels that are destinations in themselves.

Because of this, hoteliers are drawing on their imaginations and resources to create hotels that truly stand apart from the hospitality pack. There has always been a maverick spirit in America, a devil-may-care attitude to design. But now it's positively rebellious. And it's encouraging some of the most outlandish, most ambitious, most elaborate, and most extraordinary places to stay in the world. Having a hip status can often spell the beginning of the end for hotels, but in America, the hipsters just seem to get hipper.

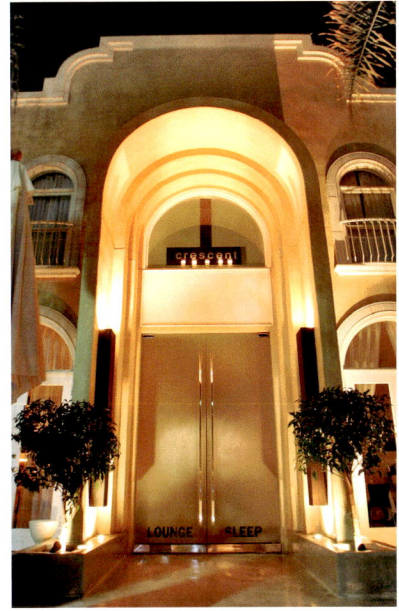

Some of the destinations that are drawing in the aesthetes include the Viceroy Santa Monica, the hotel equivalent of George Clooney with its cool-meets-playful-meets-seriously sexy interior; the Ace Hotel in Portland, a vintage-mod hotspot packed with personality and a rock'n'roll vibe (there are even vinyl turntables in the rooms); the Library Hotel in New York, where the lobby is as grand and as distinguished as the New York Library and every room is full of inspired reading (the Erotic Literature suite is very popular); the Whitelaw Hotel in Miami, a whimsical, fuschia-pink fantasy where free cocktails are offered and the slogan reads "Clean Sheets, Hot Water, Stiff Drinks"; and the Dunton Hot Springs in Colorado, where a truly remarkable retreat has been fashioned out of a former ghost town. Some places, such as Delano, have become almost as, if not more, famous than their settings, with design aficionados from around the world making the pilgrimage to the check-in desks to see what all the fuss is about.

But it's not only the architecture and style that's causing renewed interest in American hotels. It's the extras. Anxious to entertain guests and keep them coming back for more, hoteliers are conceiving ever-more enticing perks to add to their already impressive repertoire. Places such as the Viceroy Santa Monica and the Delano, The Raleigh, and the Mondrian hotels in Miami have beautifully designed, ultra-decadent, private poolside cabanas to allow you to sip your margaritas in peace, away from the public (and the paparazzi); the Hotel Victor in Miami has a Vibe Director to help you choose the music for your stay (and/or party); while Library Hotel in New York has filled both its guest rooms and its public sitting rooms with armfuls of books, so you can sit back with your favorite authors and remember the joy to be had in reading for pleasure, not for work. It's all part of the new style of finely tuned frills being offered with the top-notch service and eye-catching design. Yes indeed, hotels don't get much cooler than they do in the land of the red, white, and blue. In this country, you don't come for the sheets; you come for the show.

In the following pages, we've tried to showcase the best that America has to offer in terms of innovative hotels and edgy hideaways. We've taken the architecturally significant, the extraordinary, the slightly avant-garde, the glamorous, and the just plain deadpan cool, and collected them all up into one fabulous package of classic, contemporary, and cutting-edge hotels. Each of these inspirational destinations has been recommended by a leading architect, interior designer, editor, photographer, design critic, or travel writer, and each is notable for its design, its setting, its service, and its style. Not all are luxurious either: some are seductively simple, while others are unique retreats of such distinction, integrity, and soul, they have defiantly side-stepped the *sine qua non* of modern style in such a way that they, themselves, have become the new by-word for style.

A modern-day guide for modern-day explorers, aesthetes, A-listers, architects, style seekers, and design sophisticates, *Dream Hotels USA* is the definitive guide to getting away in the USA—and discovering great design when you get there. From the urban glamour of New York to the end-of-the-road beauty of the Florida Keys, the majestic landscapes of Montana, the Modernist cool of Palm Springs and the movie star-style drama of LA, it shows why North America is fast becoming the new Mecca for globe-trotting travelers with a keen eye for the best in fine lines and slow pleasures.

Janelle McCulloch

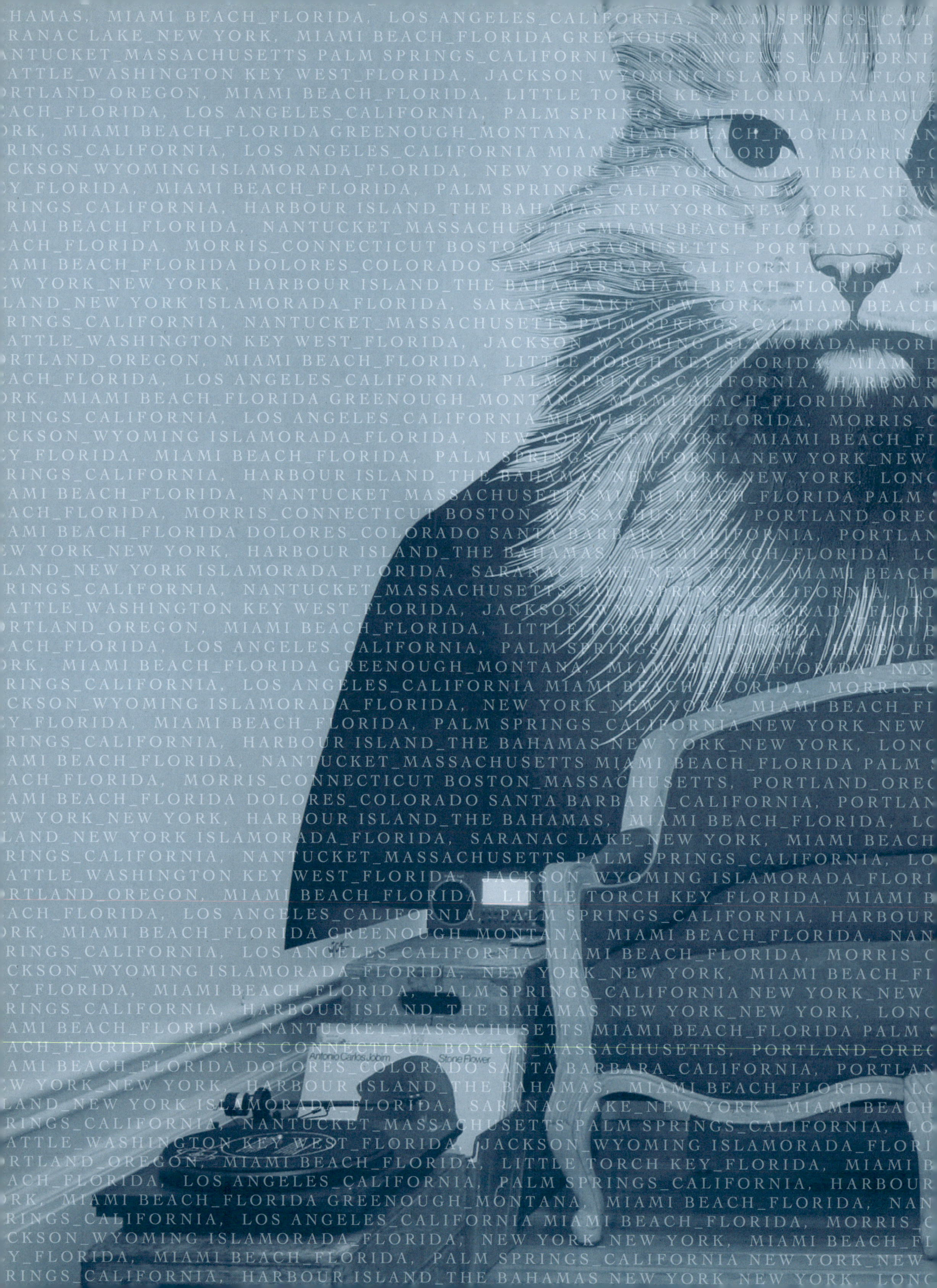

URBAN STYLE SETTERS

- Architecture/Design: Hollywood Regency
- Highlight: The poolside scene
- To pack: Your party spirit—the bar is so fabulous, you'll never want to leave

VICEROY SANTA MONICA

Santa Monica, California

Ah, the Viceroy. Just saying the name has the potential to make people swoon. It's the hotel equivalent of George Clooney—always beautiful, always cool, and always associated with the right people. The place just shimmers with style, grace, intelligence, and elegance. It's little wonder Paris Hilton tried to copy the aesthetic for her LA home.

Part of the KOR Hotels Group and designed by America's "it" designer Kelly Wearstler, queen of the ultra-hip Hollywood Regency look, this iconic Santa Monica hideaway is what its name suggests: a place of pure vice. Or, as some prefer to call it, "vice on ice." The Viceroy is undeniably Hollywood, a very "grown-up" hotel that harks back to the days of Cary Grant and Audrey Hepburn. Even the buttoned-up upholstery has a highly studied elegance. But underneath the glamour, martinis, and manners, there is another, slightly playful, side to the Viceroy. Parakeet-green Chesterfields vie for attention with walls of mirrors set in perfect compositions like wallpaper, while white, marine-vinyl daybeds slouch invitingly beside dazzling white Modernist tables. Outside in the pool area, chic, Deco-style gazebos are decked out with French dining furniture and lit at night by romantic white candelabra.

Impressed? Well, you haven't heard about the rooms, which are part *Wizard of Oz* and part *Alice in Wonderland*. Armoires are dressed in chicken-wire doors but somehow seem entirely stylish, walls are covered in lattice wallpaper that matches the parakeet-green chairs, the compositions of mirrors look oddly right—as do the compositions of white plates on the walls opposite them—and the bathrooms are marble retreats that not only hold decadent baths but gorgeous black-and-white vanity tables with Aesop toiletries.

The Viceroy Santa Monica is both an ode to crisp sophistication and a tribute to whimsical, wit-filled humor. The library, for example, is a slash of citrus yellow, the bathrooms behind the reception are tiled in a particularly vivid shade of Kelly green (and have to be seen to be believed), while the reception itself is the architectural equivalent of the little black dress—black, black, and yet more black. The cabanas, meanwhile, are dressed in carnival marquee-style licorice and white stripes, while the sleek chaise lounges, which are wrapped in white marine vinyl, are arranged in zig-zag configurations recalling a stylish still life.

All in all the hotel is completely and utterly divine, and five years after it first opened it is still the hottest hotel in town. Dress up, order one of the Viceroy's signature Key Lime martinis and prepare to feel a little bit famous for the night.

Photography courtesy KOR Hotel Group and Janelle McCulloch

- Architecture/Design: Retro with a kick
- Highlight: Everything, it's an aesthete's dream
- To pack: An open mind—Portland is a place like no other

ACE HOTEL PORTLAND
Portland, Oregon

Portland, Oregon has hit the American consciousness in recent years. The small city with a big attitude has come of age lately and is starting to flex its muscles, particularly on an aesthetic front. The place always hinted of being cool, but now it's positively hot.

One of the destinations helping to put Portland on the hipster's map is the Ace Hotel, a little gem with a lot of character. *The New York Times' T Magazine* called this vintage-mod hotspot "the country's most original," and it's easy to see why. The place is so packed with personality it almost deserves to be made into a movie. In fact, it once was: in its former life it was the Clyde Hotel, the setting for the 1989 film *Drugstore Cowboy*. With leanings toward both rock'n'roll and bohemia—Portland has a little of both in its blood—the Ace has taken hotel design and virtually reinvented it, or at least turned it on its head. It's not really like any other boutique hotel: it's more anti-boutique, and out-and-out proud of the fact too. The place is an homage to creativity and rebellious spirit.

The hotel, which is housed in an historic 1912 building, was the result of the collective imaginations of four guys, Alex Calderwood, Wade Weigel, Doug Herrick, and Jack Barron, who wanted to create a Portland space they actually wanted to spend time in. Having found the Clyde Hotel, they decided to retain many of the building's original features and fixtures in order to preserve the spirit of the old haunt, while updating the place for demanding aesthetes. They combined their artistry and the result is an ode to ingenuity. The foyer is a funky space that's reminiscent of a common room in a private boys' school, full of books and quirky touches. Staff members even look a little student-boho, with basic white shirts, pinstripe vests, skinny ties, and bike-messenger caps. There are also free MacBooks for guests to use, free wi-fi throughout the hotels, and a photo booth in the lobby, in case you need to renew your ID cards.

The rooms, which feature hand-painted murals, have salvaged timber desks and beds, and if you order a suite, you'll be rewarded with your own DJing space, including Czech-made turntables to spin your favorite records: perfect in a city famous for its love of vinyl. But perhaps the most fantastic thing about the Ace's rooms are the bathrooms, which offer luxury, deep-cast, roll-top baths to sink into while your favorite "mood music" plays in the background; they're so big you could almost have a party in the tub.

There is also a healthy respect for eco-friendliness here: some of the natural, sensitive, or recycled touches include organic cotton towels, wool army blankets, paint cans reused as waste baskets, and retro pushbikes for cruising the city. *Elle* magazine was so impressed by these things it called the place "lost-and-found fabulous." And then there's the motto under the sign on the door: "Ace: A Friendly Hotel," a cheeky reference to other hotel chains with similar but far-more-bland statements. The place is so darn gorgeous you can't help but fall in love with it.

Portland has always been a little odd, a little adolescent in its love of bohemia and being different, but that's why visitors love it. It's the younger, cooler version of Seattle, without the wealth and the overly serious business or techno geeks. Some Portland people worry that all the new attention will go to the town's head, that the media articles with headlines like "Portland Pops Off" will cause the city to be overrun with visitors, leading to the loss of its street cred. But thanks to places like the Ace, it will certainly stay cool for a good while longer. Come here, kick back, and chill out—the Ace will even supply the music for you.

Photography courtesy David Phelps and Ace Hotels

- Architecture/Design: Art Deco meets Film Noir
- Highlight: The coolly glamorous lobby
- To pack: A movie star-style wardrobe

HOTEL DELUXE
Portland, Oregon

There is something deliciously and decadently glamorous about the name Hotel deLuxe. And true to its name, this hotel is an ode to irresistible charm of the most alluring kind. It's like a flirtatious movie star who winks at you and then smiles slyly in such a way that you feel tempted to do something you perhaps shouldn't. The hotel describes the décor as having "the smile of an ingenue and the swagger of a leading man," and that's pretty close to the mark. This place puts on an unforgettable performance. Talk about striking a pose.

One of the most sophisticated hideaways in North America, the Hotel deLuxe is a place that pays homage to Hollywood. Set in the Pearl District of Portland, it emulates the opulence and style of classic movies and in the process has reinvented glamour for an age, and a generation, that has largely forgotten what the word means. The mood, the lighting, the lobby, and the bar and restaurant all come straight from either a 1940s film or a fabulous Hollywood home. It is drama of the highest caliber.

Walk in the front door and you feel as though you should be wearing Dior and carrying Louis Vuitton bags. Coolly glamorous, the hotel features a rotating cycle of vintage film stills, wall-size photographs of old stars, black-and-white photos of 1930s, '40s, and '50s movies, sweeping staircases that Scarlett O'Hara would have loved, crystal chandeliers, gilded gold accents on the ceiling, and floor-to-ceiling curtains that look beautifully ballgown-ish. The restaurant is called Gracie's and features sharkskin chairs and faux-marble pillars, while the Driftwood Room is a noirish place to practice your Humphrey Bogart/Lauren Bacall pose. Rooms are just as lovely, with buttery leather headboards and Art Deco Lucite lamps, and the hotel even caters for pets—just in case your entourage of diamond-collared poodles wants to come too. Elizabeth Taylor would love it.

In fact, it's all so fabulous that it's difficult to believe the place was once an historic but ever-so-slightly rundown hotel. The $10-million renovation worked liked an LA surgeon on an aging star, imparting an Art Deco-meets-Noir-style ambiance that seems so perfect that it's a wonder why no hotelier has ever thought of it before. To continue the Hollywood theme, each floor is devoted to filmmakers or stars—Hitchcock has his own floor, Fellini and Bergman are on Six. Film buffs tend to love it. To satisfy modern travelers, however, there are also modern touches: iPod docking stations, a 24-hour gym, and a spiritual menu (your choice of religious text). It's a hotel with attitude but it's a good attitude. It treats guests like stars and the first-class service seems to work—nobody has thrown a diva fit yet.

Photography courtesy David Phelps

Architecture/Design: Pared-back minimalism
Highlight: Next to the price, the Belltown location; Seattle's most fashionable neighborhood
To pack: A warm wrap or coat, preferably one as stylish as the rooms

ACE HOTEL SEATTLE

Seattle, Washington DC

Seattle is a little like Portland, its smaller sister to the south, and not just in terms of climate. Both cities often suffer from being overlooked by an international travel crowd that tends to be more concerned with LA, New York, San Francisco, or Miami. Both cities have carved out their own styles: Portland within the music and design scenes and Seattle within the coffee and technology arena. And both cities are not afraid to show their quirky personalities. These cities pride themselves on their oddities (it's precisely these oddities that have made these places so individual) and if you pay a visit to either one, you'll see why they are starting to earn a lot of respect for standing up and daring to be different.

Taking a cue from this rebellious stance are Seattle's new-wave hotels, which are currently pushing the hospitality envelope in terms of design and style. One of the most talked-about is the Ace Hotel, a hipper-than-hip little place that's raising eyebrows for both its aesthetic statement and its happening "scene." The Ace bills itself as a place for people "looking for more than just a room." It says it wants to make guests feel like they are "somewhere" rather than anywhere—and they are indeed somewhere: in Belltown, the city's trendiest neighborhood. But it's inside, however, where they *really* know they're somewhere a little different.

Loved by twenty- and thirty-somethings who come to Seattle to party in style, the hotel has geared itself toward such hipsters by drenching itself in layers of white-on-white minimalism—white wood floors, white brick walls, white moldings, white foyer—and then added fantastic accessories to catch the eye. The most wonderfully eccentric of these accessories are the murals—enormous, cover-the-wall 1970s photomurals of the Pacific Northwest's great outdoors—that lead you to wonder if you're in Seattle or somewhere upstate. The platform beds are also a little "rustic hut"; they were salvaged from overseas hotels in the Ace's admirable recycling/eco-conscious style, while the gray wool blankets are from the French military, the hallway carpet is a coconut husk material, and the bathrooms are furnished in stainless-steel sinks. It's the industrial look meets Mother Nature. It's also a bit of a surprise in Seattle, where everything else is quite high-tech. And the low-key charm seems to work. The hotel is packed out with young things day and night, most of them ready to celebrate, so if you're staying at the Ace don't plan on going to bed early.

The idea for the Ace Hotels venture came about when architects Wade Weigel and Alex Calderwood and designer Eric Hentz came together to create an inexpensive place to stay in Seattle that still had a good vibe. Their philosophy was to offer a place to friends and guests that stayed under the $100 price range, but still had loads to offer in terms of position and style. The architects took a former run-down boarding house and, keeping much of the configuration, made the small spaces seem larger with high ceilings, low beds, and minimal but carefully selected furnishings, with a few extra witty details to amuse and delight. The benches came from Thonet, for example, via Boeing, which had once used them in an airport, while the rooms each feature a copy of the Kama Sutra rather than a bible. Cheeky indeed.

It is the sort of austere yet spirited place rock bands love—there are even bunk rooms for bands to stay in—fused with street culture and Seattle style. It's a mix of natural and man-made, new and found, high-end and low. And it's become an instant hit with aspiring young web designers, documentary directors, and musicians. There's a saying in this city: "No starch please; we're from Seattle." It absolutely applies here, at the Ace Hotel.

Photography courtesy David Phelps and Janelle McCulloch

LIBRARY HOTEL

New York, New York

What is it about books and libraries that fascinates people so? Both have always been coveted, but in recent years they've become such a fashionable asset that even hotels are incorporating libraries into their design. One of them, the Library Hotel, has gone so far as to design an entire New York hotel around the concept.

Inspired by New York's love of reading and also its neighbors, the landmark New York Public Library and the Pierpont Morgan Library, the Library Hotel is an ode to books. The foyer is a handsome, grand, bookshelf-enhanced space; the Writer's Den/Poetry Garden Terrace has more books, plus a fireplace to curl up and read beside in utter luxury; and the Reading Room is simply an enormous, irresistible space, complete with courtesy wine and cheese, in which to while away the afternoon. In all, The Library is home to more than 6,000 books.

If that's not inspiration enough, each floor and room is categorized according to the Dewey Decimal system. Each floor is based on a theme—for example, Languages, Technology, The Arts, Philosophy—and each room is based on a subject matter—Architecture, Photography, Fashion, Classics. Inside each of these rooms is a bookshelf full of great reading, so that all you need to do is fill up the deep bath in the enormous ensuite, slip on the Do Not Disturb sign, and relax with one or several of these intriguing volumes.

The most popular room, predictably, is Erotic Literature, although there are stories of books slipping into other rooms late at night—Casanova's memoirs somehow ended up one morning in an adjoining suite. Many guests, of course, prefer to choose rooms containing their favorite topics—Neil Armstrong stayed in the Astronomy room. It is a stroke of design genius because there's a book lover in all of us, and even those who don't read are still impressed by the sight of this very "smart" hotel.

Conceived by hotelier Henry Kallan, the hotel was originally a turn-of-the-century building with beautiful detailing, including a copper bay window that extends the length of the façade and a fabulous view of Madison Avenue. Kallan, no slouch when it comes to research himself, realized that the gimmick of having a library-style hotel wasn't enough: it needed to have a little Manhattan luxury and comfort as well. So the furniture is a mix of elegant ebony tables and soft leather banquettes, the décor includes champagne wallpaper and mahogany doors and cabinetry, and the rooms feature indulgent bathrooms with deep tubs. All in all, it has the feel of a private club that's sophisticated but also a little sensual. The entire hotel is as quiet as a public library and is a welcome sliver of calm in the middle of noisy Manhattan.

Photography courtesy Janelle McCulloch and Library Hotel

- Architecture/Design: Black-and-white glamour
- Highlight: The Gothic lobby
- To pack: Lots of black, of course!

NIGHT
New York, New York

With New York being one of the world's style capitals, you'd think that more hotels there would be a little more experimental when it comes to architecture and design. After all, if anyone's going to accept edginess, it's a New Yorker. But sadly, the majority of places to stay in Manhattan are grand old hotels that often need a facelift, bland hotel chains that feature equally bland interiors, or cramped guesthouses that have more chintz than chic. A handful of hoteliers, however, are choosing to show a little New York style by going against the design grain and producing destinations with some kick. One of them is Night. So cool, it's known by one word, this very Gothic, very Gothamesqe study in urban drama was conceived by energetic young entrepreneur Vikram Chatwal, who had already cut his teeth on the Time and Dream hotels nearby (also his; also just as funky).

Night, a former Best Western around the corner from Times Square, was not only in a prime position, with the hip QT hotel across the road, but also small enough to be a canvas for some truly creative designing. What Chatwal decided to do was take with New York's favorite shade, black. It all fitted—the name (New York and particularly Times Square are fabulous at night); the shade (think of New York fashion; of things like Batman's black cape); and even the style, which treads a dramatic line between modern and oh-my-God. Few journalists know how to describe the interior, other than to say it's seriously sexy; even the slogan reads "Fantasize, Flavors, Frolicking, Fetish." Don't come here if you're at all shy.

Walk in to the hotel and the first thing that confronts you is a series of erotic black-and-white photographs in the style of Helmut Newton, the second thing is the cow-hide sofa, the third the black-and-white leather chairs. If, after these things, you're still looking to be impressed, well, there are the black-and-white books set in perfect black-and-white lines behind the front desk, the enormous Gothic armoire, the bar at the back, and the film noir-style lighting and atmosphere. Okay, so some of the hotel is quite dark—pitch black, in fact—but once you adjust your eyes, it's very sexy.

The rooms have been criticized as being small, but they actually feel more spacious than standard New York rooms and are packed with design features to amuse you for the length of your stay. Beds are a mix of sleigh and high style, with elongated headboards and platform bases resting on stainless-steel legs. The desks are pieces that hedge fund executives

would admire and are enhanced with nickel lamps and fabulously soft leather armchairs. There is also a black bed stool in each room, a plush white bathrobe in a cupboard lined with black-and-white wallpaper, and charcoal-black bathrooms with Kohler rainshower heads and Frette towels. Oh—and plasma screen TVs, Bose stereos, and black iPod Nanos.

Night is far more than a collection of cute black assets though. It is an ode to fantasia. Outrageous while still being composed, and in-your-face while still understated, it combines contrasts in a way that's rare in the hotel world. Normally, hotel designers stick with one style, but Night takes a more perverse view. Why have one when you can try them all?

It is all very over the top, of course, but that's partly why it works. The foyer is perpetually full of models and black-suited Frenchmen, the doormen are cheeky and charming in the same breath, the rooms are entertainment in themselves, and the area is ripe to be explored. Night or day, this hotel has everything you need. As the hotel says: "Desire it at night? So it shall be…"

Photography courtesy Night and Janelle McCulloch

- Architecture/Design: SoHo loft
- Highlight: The bathrooms—some of the best in America
- To pack: A small camera—the celebrity spotting is famous

THE MERCER

SoHo, New York

André Balazs's hotels always seem to attract a lot of attention, and not just for their design. It was in The Mercer that Russell Crowe was arrested for third-degree assault for throwing a phone at a member of staff. It is in The Mercer where designer Marc Jacobs likes to retire to escape his critics—the hotel has been his unofficial residence since 1998. And it is in The Mercer where a great many stars elect to do interviews for their upcoming books, films, and TV series, both so that they can appear cool and so that they can take sneak peeks at all the other celebrities who are usually floating around the foyer. When actress Julianne Nicholson once gave an interview to a *USA Today* writer, she spotted Elvis Costello strolling through and immediately went ga-ga right in front of the journalist. "Now *that*," she sighed, "is a celebrity sighting. The other day, I saw Ben Kingsley. This hotel is ridiculous."

Located on the corner of the perennially stylish Mercer and Prince Streets, in the thick of New York's SoHo district, the hotel may be known for its star sightings but it also deserves a few ticks for its design. Inspired by the area's loft architecture, Balazs decided to reconfigure the Romanesque Revival building, built in 1890 for tycoon John Jacob Astor, that was based on the industrial-chic style that had become so popular with residents renovating the surrounding apartments. It was an inspired move. He kept the ceiling heights, the windows, and the impressive scale of the warehouse-style space, which also retained the natural light and the views, and then enhanced the industrial assets by exposing brickwork and using iron support columns to heighten the feel of living in a loft. Those rooms that had working fireplaces kept their working fireplaces, while the beautiful, enormous arched windows in the loft suite on the top floor made for a penthouse with a difference.

By leaving much of the architecture intact, Balazs not only kept the New York–SoHo flavor of the building but also created a sense of hype. No other New York hotel had tried to emulate Manhattan style in this way, and both locals and visitors embraced it at first sight. Added to the drama was the fact that Parisian designer Christian Liaigre had been commissioned to do the rooms in his signature simplicity and Wenge-wood elegance. All the ingredients were set for a hotel hit. Then all Balazs needed to do was dust in some celebrities, which Balazs does well anyway, and success was ensured. The place has been buzzing ever since. Even Russell Crowe hasn't been able to put a dint in The Mercer's reputation.

The key to The Mercer is that it provides a little sliver of calm in an otherwise frenzied city. The rooms have been designed in a subtle, streamlined way and are surprisingly serene; the marble bathrooms are like mini day spas; the restaurant, Kitchen, is deliberately casual; and the library–lounge and lobby are such easy and relaxing spaces to be in that you can see why celebrities idle through unperturbed by public attention. There are even collections of books on display for you to flick through while you're waiting for your publicist to appear. This pared-down establishment has a gallery-like silence and glamour that immediately appeals. Even the staff, dressed as they are in their sexy uniforms, are as helpful as old friends: they'll fetch anything for you. Even a new phone, if need be.

Photography courtesy The Mercer

- Architecture/Design: Discreet sophistication
- Highlight: The grand duplex suites
- To pack: A lover—it's a place you want to hide away in

CITY CLUB HOTEL
New York, New York

With so many hotels flooding the global market, and especially in New York City where they seem to crowd every corner, hoteliers are finding that something different is needed to attract guests. One of the tricks being used by younger hoteliers is the private club atmosphere, one that is cozy, intimate, personal, and memorable. Lobbies are kept deliberately small and have a residential feel, while rooms often vary in style, with personal touches such as antique maps, flowers, artwork, and living areas that feel more like home than your own.

New York's City Club Hotel is one such place. Originally a club for politically minded gentlemen, the 105-year-old building was bought by Jeff Klein and converted into a small, 65-room hotel. Klein wanted a cozy feel for the hotel, rather than what's known in the trade as S & M (Standing and Modeling), an activity that often goes on in fashionable hotels. He wanted a place that guests could feel immediately at home in as soon as they walked in the door. So Klein hired designer Jeffrey Bilhuber to remodel the rooms, with the brief that they should feel sophisticated but also intimate and homely.

The color scheme of the City Club is based on a very distinguished mix of chocolate, beige, and pale-blue, but each room is slightly different in personality. There are vintage books, vinyl records, fabulous artwork, Frette linens, Hermès toiletries to play with, and staff members who remember your name—even though they're wearing Paul Smith uniforms and look far too sexy to be waiting on you. There are blankets with "City Club" woven into them to add to the gentleman's club feel, and there are even vintage postcards scattered about the place.

It is all very clubby, and all very cool, but without the snob factor. And presiding over it all is the head of the house himself, Mr. Klein, who's quite pleased with the way his vision has turned out. The hotel is an ode to his version of good living, and every detail—from the Fifth Avenue-style residence aesthetic to the free soft drinks in the mini-bar—are his touch. Klein wanted to create a place with soul, that cosseted and comforted while it inspired, and the City Club does all that and more.

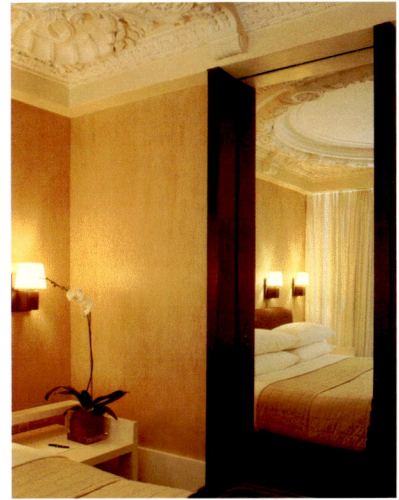

The most stylish parts of the City Club are the three grand duplex suites, which were carved out of the old 20-foot-high ballroom. Each of these spaces is like a small hotel in itself. With the original ornate ceilings and enormous Palladian windows as the elegant shells, the suites reflect a quiet grandeur. Circular staircases rise up to mezzanine bedrooms and oversized, chocolate-marble bathrooms, quirky works of art provide additional interest, and plush, book-filled living rooms provide a comforting space to come home to after a hard day's business in New York City.

It's not surprising that Klein designed such a retreat: the globetrotter grew up in places like The Connaught and Claridge's and still vacations in destinations prefaced with Aman. He knows what works and what doesn't in hotels, and he's determined not to let others' mistakes invade his oh-so-personal Manhattan hideaway. There is something of a gentlemanly courtesy about Klein, just as there is about his hotel: it's as if all the gentlemen guests of the past have lingered on, casting an approving glance over the new place. Unlike the old place, however, you don't need a membership to enjoy the experience.

Photography courtesy City Club Hotel

- Architecture/Design: Pretty in pink
- Highlight: The music and vibe
- To pack: Your dancing shoes—there's a DJ in the lobby

WHITELAW HOTEL
Miami, Florida

It is easy to fall in love with the Whitelaw Hotel. It's a little more difficult to know why. It may be the acres of fuschia pink everywhere, so unexpected in a hotel and yet so perfect in this location, set in the heart of pink-loving Miami. It may be the quirky lobby, which is one part dance club with a live DJ spinning tunes most of the day, one part bar with a bartender offering cocktails as soon as you walk in (complimentary from 7 to 8 pm), and one part sheer whimsy, with high-backed, white-painted Victorian chairs and black crystal chandeliers offering a sense of wicked drama right from the outset. Or it may simply be the decadent humor, reflected in everything from the offbeat "do not disturb" signs—magnetic strips you throw on the outside of your door that say either "Shhhhh" or "Clean Up"—to the slogan, which reads: "Clean Sheets; Hot Water; Stiff Drinks." Talk about a hotel with personality.

Set on Collins Avenue, half a block back from the action of Ocean Drive, the hotel was conceived as a one-stop party scene. The atmosphere here is firmly social, and the vibe is loud and proud. It's a place for people who want character and cocktails in equal measure, and most of the guests here are as fun as the hotel itself. The place isn't necessarily luxe—the bathrooms are small and the cute retro linoleum floors surprise some people—but the hotel has a decidedly fun attitude that wins you over anyway.

The hotel bills itself as "a place that transports its guests into a world unique from any other Miami Beach accommodations," and for all the boasting it's not far off the mark. But the thing about the Whitelaw Hotel is that it's not all superficial style and shallow living—there is actually a lot of substance beneath the cocktails and cheek. For example, the distinctive rooms feature things that you wouldn't normally find in hotels such as this. The beds are dressed in luxurious white Belgian sheets, which look surprisingly elegant against headboards and walls decorated in fuschia pink and white, and each of the rooms has an enormous plasma television, well-stocked fridges, and funky stereo systems, so you can create your own party before you head out for the evening.

The Whitelaw Hotel works because its owner Alan Lieberman, who also owns the Chesterfield across the road (the same whimsical décor, only in black and white), The Shelley a few doors down, and a scattering of other destinations under his South Beach boutique hotel group, understands that a majority of people traveling to Miami want the fantasy of Miami as much as the reality. They want the sins and the wicked humor and the tantalizing lifestyle. They want the wannabe models and the DJs and dancers and they long to see some action too, be it celebrity-flecked or simply SoBe drama. It's the glitz and the glamour people come to South Beach for, argues Lieberman, and with the Whitelaw Hotel he has happily given it to them.

Photography courtesy Janelle McCulloch

THE SAGAMORE

Miami, Florida

The Sagamore has all the hallmarks of a great hotel—a legendary one, in fact. Originally built in 1948, it is encased in a gracious white Modernist façade, and while some of the Deco interior has been lost, in its place is a hotel that still shimmers of style—and a lot of intrigue.

Renovated in 2002, The Sagamore's raison d'etre is as a stately upmarket luxury hideaway, but it also serves as a kind of "living gallery" full of artwork and other fascinating pieces. The latter stops it from becoming too stuffy, too dull, and also gives guests something to look at when they're not busy ogling all the equally gorgeous guests. Both the guests and the other pieces of eye candy are worth seeing here. In fact, The Sagamore vies with the best galleries for its collection of contemporary works.

Set out with the same clean lines as a gallery—even the floors and walls are done in glossy white—the hotel extends down to the beach via an elongated space peppered with artwork. There are busts mounted on modern columns, electronic installations that greet you as you wander into the place, and huge, organically shaped chairs to slink into and take it all in. The hotel even has its own curator to coordinate the plethora of pieces by more than two-dozen international artists.

But the hotel isn't just a gallery showcasing hip, contemporary artists, it's a showpiece of style on all levels. The predominantly white interior stretches out via a black-and-white restaurant to a green-and-white outdoor area, where low-slung white chairs and green-and-white-striped banquettes provide some of the most sophisticated seating in Miami. The white market umbrellas, sexy banquettes, gray rattan beach chairs, and green hedges sit together in such a way it's as if a landscape designer and an architect worked closely together to create a scene of perfect symmetry. The pool is a similar pleasure zone for the eyes, with gray modern deckchairs done like natural "pods" and slick white cabanas.

It's all very dreamy and far less crowded with posers than other hauteur-then-thou hotels in South Beach. It's a grown-up kind of place; an anti-hip, anti-hedonistic hideaway that still manages to be heavenly, decadent, mysterious and magical at the same time. You can't quite put your finger on it but The Sagamore has that certain something that makes hotels ultra special.

Photography courtesy Janelle McCulloch and Eric Laignal

- Architecture/Design: H_2O-focused
- Highlight: The outdoor areas
- To pack: Tension—it will be massaged away here

THE STANDARD, MIAMI
Miami, Florida

There is nothing ordinary about The Standard hotels. In fact, they're so far from standard that they are widely recognized as being some of the most unique in North America. Conceived by hotelier and celebrity mix-master André Balazs, these inexpensive but thoroughly distinct hideaways are noted for their edgy architecture and eye-raising interior design. The Standard in downtown LA, for example, features a human fish tank where a model poses for guests while they check in, rooms that are priced according to their titles—XLarge, Huge, Gigantic, or Humongous—and air-conditioning controls that range from Blow to Hard/Harder, and Stop. Subtle, they aren't. The Standard slant is very much on entertainment—of every kind.

With The Standard in Miami, however, a new, improved, and decidedly mature Standard model has emerged from the party. Distinctly different from her LA sisters, the Miami version is far more mature in feel, although vestiges of the party-loving spirit still linger. There are still wicked details everywhere, and frankly a Standard wouldn't be a Standard without them. The rooms, for example, range from Missionary to Dry, Lush, Wet, and Full Spread. Evidently, this is not a place to take your grandmother, but there is also a surprising level sophistication to be found here on this small island off Miami.

Focusing on wellbeing through water, the hotel has been designed around the idea of rejuvenation. Wet and Full Spread rooms have roll-top baths to collapse in after a few days of clubbing, the outdoor infinity pool—a wet-edge pleasure square with one of the best views of the sea in this city—has underwater music and high-pressure jets to get you swimming laps, the Arctic plunge pool wakes you up from a hangover, the classic cedar sauna and steam room expunge all the toxins, and the Turkish *hammam* and Roman waterfall hot tub makes you feel like one piece again.

The Standard, Miami is officially a wellness centre, but really, it's a spa with sass. It aspires to revive (and redefine) bathhouse culture, but in a way that's healthy rather than naughty—although some of these treatments are downright decadent. Even the spa menu has saucy and suggestive names—The Standard Spanking, for example, involves a massaging of the buttocks. There are also outdoor yoga lawns, a garden fire lounge, a mud lounge (clothing optional), acupuncture sessions, workshops, meditation, Tai Chi, an aroma steam room, Pilates, and a naturopathic clinic. Some guests have commented that it is a place to go to party, and then recover, all in the same hotel.

The most unusual thing about The Standard, Miami, though, is the design. For such a lavish place, the architecture is almost Scandinavian in simplicity. Spaces are pared-down to the point of being almost minimalist. Rooms have all-white walls, sandy tones, and natural wood furnishings, the *hammam* is all-marble, the lobby has the serenity of a library, the breakfast area is on a slatted wood deck overlooking Biscayne Bay, and the contemplative courtyard a space to sit and think in complete peace. The use of mobile phones is strongly discouraged here, enabling guests to switch off and relax. If you want noise and conversation, well, Miami Beach is just across the bay.

It's terribly stylish, but it's also terribly clever. Balazs has done it again with this hotel. The Standard, Miami is like a good dose of hangover potion after a big night of partying: a hotel that simultaneously revives and inspires.

Photography courtesy The Standard

- Architecture/Design: Dignified
- Highlight: The poolside cabanas
- To pack: Something to chill out in

THE CHAMBERLAIN

West Hollywood, California

When it opened, The Chamberlain created an immediate stir within the media. Part of this fuss centered on the interior design, which was significantly different from most hotels. It was more like a private home than a commercial business, an atmosphere enhanced by both the tree-lined residential West Hollywood neighborhood and the slogan: "In Town, In Residence, In Style." Staying at the hotel was like moving to Hollywood without paying the huge mortgage. Several years on, The Chamberlain is still being used as a private retreat by its adoring guests, and although the small size isn't for everyone, the sweetness and elegance of the destination does entice.

The inspiration to transform The Chamberlain into an intimate hotel came from the building's former life as an 1970s apartment block—the four-story property still has that cozy feel, only now it's less bland and a lot more upmarket. The décor was designed by Kelly Wearstler, who also did the Viceroy, so the same lovely, plumped-up English feel is there—gracious grays and blues enhance the clubby mood while buttoned sofas and add to the eccentric but expensive look.

The rooms are the kind you'd find in a wealthy household in Beverly Hills or a country house in England, with Mascioni 250-count sheets, gas-log fireplace, and stylish desks to write your thank-you letters on. There are also separate living and sleeping areas—all very civilized. Where The Chamberlain has really made a splash though is with the rooftop pool, which has touches of the Viceroy's black-and-white glamour, but is more subtle and less ostentatious. There are cabanas if you prefer privacy, but The Chamberlain is more about mixing it with others. And besides, if you hide yourself away, you'll miss the spectacular panoramas of LA and the Hollywood Hills. The bar and restaurant downstairs are also good for a kickback session and are designed to evoke the stylish home of a well-traveled host. At The Chamberlain it's easy to forget you were ever in a hotel.

It's not a flashy place, which is surprising for both LA and this area, but this deliberate refusal to subscribe to the glammed-up, red-carpet-style look is a lovely breath of fresh air. Wearstler describes The Chamberlain as "modern luxe," but it's probably more down-to-earth luxe. It's a place to lay one's head without worrying about whether one is cool enough to do so.

Photography courtesy Janelle McCulloch

■ Architecture/Design: Playfully chic
■ Highlight: The price—and the beach a few steps away
■ To pack: A swimsuit and flip-flops

TOWNHOUSE HOTEL
Miami Beach, Florida

Tucked away in a little street that leads straight to SoBe's famous beach, the Townhouse Hotel has to be one of Miami's best-kept secrets. It's not totally secret, of course—big-name brands such as Elle, Hugo Boss, and Nike have used its gloriously cheeky interiors and rooftop as a backdrop for photo shoots over the past few years—but it's still considered something of a "find" among the design cognoscenti, who pass its name on in hushed tones. The Townhouse has been described by reviewers as "mischievous" and a "big adult playhouse," and those descriptions are pretty apt—a stay at this hotel is like going back to your childhood playroom and mucking about, only with far more sophisticated things to play with.

To start with there's the reception area, although with the front desk discreetly tucked into a corner it's less of a reception area and more of a gallery of fun. There's a row of red and white bikes waiting to be used, a generous scattering of red and white chairs to lounge in, an oversized mirror to check your posing, a big photographer's spotlight, and a welcoming, sun-lit dining area/sunroom. Full of white chairs with red-and-white cushions, it's a great place to grab some breakfast or catch up on the latest design magazines and newspapers. Upstairs, on the rooftop terrace, there's another cheeky play area with low-slung red daybeds sheltered by red market umbrellas and a splendid view of Miami around you. Not surprisingly it has become one of the most popular places to be on summer nights and weekends when the rooftop bar is open.

The rooms, meanwhile, are slightly pared-down in comparison to the rest of the hotel and feature bleached whitewashed floorboards, L-shaped couches, red flower lampshades, fire-engine-red telephones, white beds with baby blue pillows, and cherry-red plastic beach balls instead of chocolates on the pillows. The Townhouse feels like a private beach house and most guests treat it as such, happily kicking back in the living areas and helping themselves to the open kitchen, free magazines, and sun-drenched rooftop area.

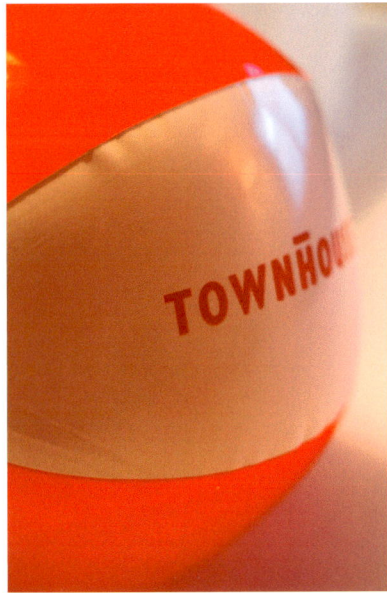

The hotel was designed by Parisian designer India Madhavi, whose whimsical design graces every corner of this playful establishment. Even the front porch is decked out with red swings and cute chairs to stretch out on. If you want to take some of the Townhouse's cheeriness home with you, the hotel's signature beach balls, towels, and other playful paraphernalia can be purchased behind the front desk.

Photography courtesy Janelle McCulloch

OWNHOUS

ROOFTOP

BOND ST
LOUNGE

Architecture/Design: Miami cool
Highlight: The atmosphere—this place is party central
To pack: A sense of fun

THE CATALINA
Miami Beach, Florida

Part of the South Beach Group, a name as famous for its party scenes as is for its startling design and architecture, The Catalina Hotel & Beach Club is one of Miami Beach's most eye-popping hideaways. Decked out in red and white—and myriad other colors—it has been described by many reviewers as Austin Powersish, and the similarities are certainly there. The place is one part groovy and one pure, well, groovier. A Disney animator couldn't have come up with a cooler, more colorful, more cartoonish interior. Think red shag carpet, bright red sofas, more red chairs, and occasional spots of bright white to break it all up. And that's just in the main foyer—the other areas have their own personality altogether.

Located in front of the famous Raleigh Hotel on Collins Avenue and just down from the equally famous Delano, The Catalina had to do something unique to set itself apart from the SoBe hotel crowd. The hotel consists of three buildings—The Catalina as the main building with the Dorset and Maxine buildings directly to the side. It's smaller in height than the Big Boys across the road, but that doesn't matter as it's easily identifiable by all the cars pulling up outside, the people milling about around the two restaurants (Kung Fu Kitchen & Sushi and Maxine's Bistro & Bar), and the façade of the foyer, which exudes the faint air of a Broadway theater. Enormous windows framed by white flowing drapes stretch up two levels to the double-height ceiling, while the sitting area itself looks like a stage set with funky white-leather mini sofas and ottomans, crafted wooden stools, and an enormous red rug. But while it seems all very Miamiesque and fabulously over-the-top, The Catalina is actually very friendly, and, unlike some other hotels, welcomes you whether you're a movie star or a tourist in town for two days. In fact, like its sister hotel the Whitelaw, it offers free Happy Hour from 7 pm to 8 pm, which makes the atmosphere even livelier and more hospitable.

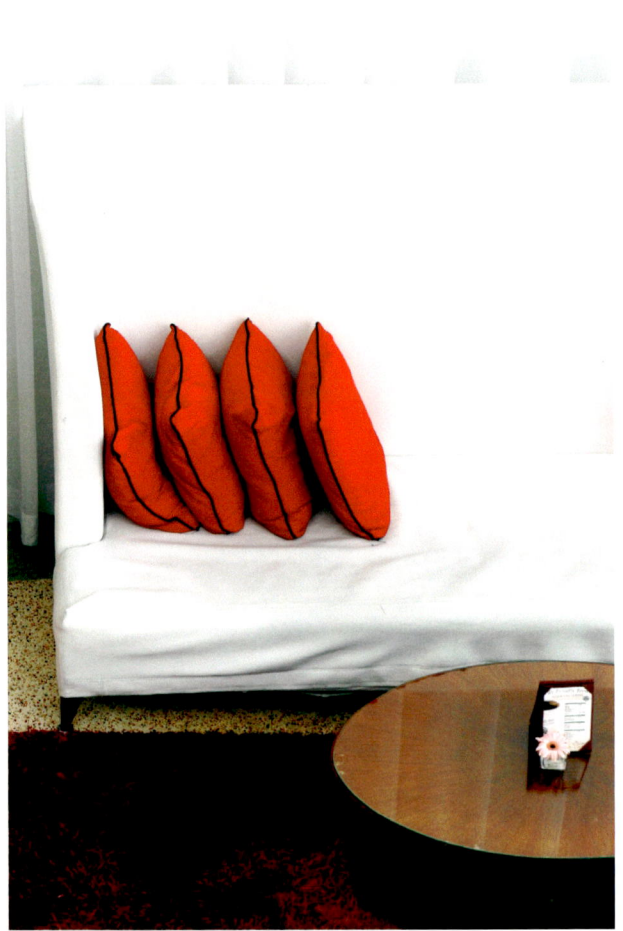

Away from the flamboyant foyer, the spaces are a little quieter but no less intriguing. There's a bamboo garden that serves as a serene retreat when the front-of-house and street-side ambience becomes too much, a 75-foot pool and covered chaise longues to recover from that Ocean Drive hangover, and finally a rooftop area—although that's really where the party gets going after a certain post-midnight hour! The rooms feature intriguing touches, too. The Standard rooms are decorated with white floorboards, white beds, and white chaise longues that are offset by tomato-red lampshades, while the Dorset suites are like chocolate boxes, with rich brown baroque wallpaper, crystal chandeliers, and elegant faux-Louis chairs. Each room also comes with Tempur-Pedic Swedish Mattresses, 300-thread count Mascioni sheets, goose-down comforters and pillows, and flatscreen TVs.

The Catalina Hotel & Beach Club has a lot of the South Beach Group's personality flowing through the hotel, but you can also get away from the party if you need to. And as an unexpected bonus, the price is perfect for those seeking style and design on a modest budget.

Photography courtesy Janelle McCulloch

BARBARA_CALIFORNIA, PORTLAND_OREGON, MIAMI BEACH_FLORIDA, LITTLE TORCH
HAMAS, MIAMI BEACH_FLORIDA, LOS ANGELES_CALIFORNIA, PALM SPRINGS_CALI
RANAC LAKE_NEW YORK, MIAMI BEACH_FLORIDA GREENOUGH_MONTANA, MIAMI B
NANTUCKET_MASSACHUSETTS PALM SPRINGS_CALIFORNIA, LOS ANGELES_CALIFORNI
EATTLE_WASHINGTON KEY WEST_FLORIDA, JACKSON_WYOMING ISLAMORADA_FLOR
ORTLAND_OREGON, MIAMI BEACH_FLORIDA, LITTLE TORCH KEY_FLORIDA, MIAMI
EACH_FLORIDA, LOS ANGELES_CALIFORNIA, PALM SPRINGS_CALIFORNIA, HARBOUR
ORK, MIAMI BEACH_FLORIDA GREENOUGH_MONTANA, MIAMI BEACH_FLORIDA, NAN
RINGS_CALIFORNIA, LOS ANGELES_CALIFORNIA MIAMI BEACH_FLORIDA, MORRIS_C
CKSON_WYOMING ISLAMORADA_FLORIDA, NEW YORK_NEW YORK, MIAMI BEACH_FL
EY_FLORIDA, MIAMI BEACH_FLORIDA, PALM SPRINGS_CALIFORNIA NEW YORK_NEW
RINGS_CALIFORNIA, HARBOUR ISLAND_THE BAHAMAS NEW YORK_NEW YORK, LONG
IAMI BEACH_FLORIDA, NANTUCKET_MASSACHUSETTS MIAMI BEACH_FLORIDA PALM
EACH_FLORIDA, MORRIS_CONNECTICUT BOSTON_MASSACHUSETTS, PORTLAND_ORE
IAMI BEACH_FLORIDA DOLORES_COLORADO SANTA BARBARA_CALIFORNIA, PORTLAN
EW YORK_NEW YORK, HARBOUR ISLAND_THE BAHAMAS, MIAMI BEACH_FLORIDA, LO
LAND_NEW YORK ISLAMORADA_FLORIDA, SARANAC LAKE_NEW YORK, MIAMI BEACH
RINGS_CALIFORNIA, NANTUCKET_MASSACHUSETTS PALM SPRINGS_CALIFORNIA, LO
EATTLE_WASHINGTON KEY WEST_FLORIDA, JACKSON_WYOMING ISLAMORADA_FLORI
ORTLAND_OREGON, MIAMI BEACH_FLORIDA, LITTLE TORCH KEY_FLORIDA, MIAMI
EACH_FLORIDA, LOS ANGELES_CALIFORNIA, PALM SPRINGS_CALIFORNIA, HARBOU
ORK, MIAMI BEACH_FLORIDA GREENOUGH_MONTANA, MIAMI BEACH_FLORIDA, NAN
RINGS_CALIFORNIA, LOS ANGELES_CALIFORNIA MIAMI BEACH_FLORIDA, MORRIS_C
CKSON_WYOMING ISLAMORADA_FLORIDA, NEW YORK_NEW YORK, MIAMI BEACH_FL
EY_FLORIDA, MIAMI BEACH_FLORIDA, PALM SPRINGS_CALIFORNIA NEW YORK_NEW
RINGS_CALIFORNIA, HARBOUR ISLAND_THE BAHAMAS NEW YORK_NEW YORK, LONG
IAMI BEACH_FLORIDA, NANTUCKET_MASSACHUSETTS MIAMI BEACH_FLORIDA PALM
EACH_FLORIDA, MORRIS_CONNECTICUT BOSTON_MASSACHUSETTS, PORTLAND_ORE
IAMI BEACH_FLORIDA DOLORES_COLORADO SANTA BARBARA_CALIFORNIA, PORTLAN
EW YORK_NEW YORK, HARBOUR ISLAND_THE BAHAMAS, MIAMI BEACH_FLORIDA, LO
LAND_NEW YORK ISLAMORADA_FLORIDA, SARANAC LAKE_NEW YORK, MIAMI BEACH
RINGS_CALIFORNIA, NANTUCKET_MASSACHUSETTS PALM SPRINGS_CALIFORNIA, LO
EATTLE_WASHINGTON KEY WEST_FLORIDA, JACKSON_WYOMING ISLAMORADA_FLOR
ORTLAND_OREGON, MIAMI BEACH_FLORIDA, LITTLE TORCH KEY_FLORIDA, MIAMI
EACH_FLORIDA, LOS ANGELES_CALIFORNIA, PALM SPRINGS_CALIFORNIA, HARBOU
ORK, MIAMI BEACH_FLORIDA GREENOUGH_MONTANA, MIAMI BEACH_FLORIDA, NAN
RINGS_CALIFORNIA, LOS ANGELES_CALIFORNIA MIAMI BEACH_FLORIDA, MORRIS_C
CKSON_WYOMING ISLAMORADA_FLORIDA, NEW YORK_NEW YORK, MIAMI BEACH_FL
EY_FLORIDA, MIAMI BEACH_FLORIDA, PALM SPRINGS_CALIFORNIA NEW YORK_NEW
RINGS_CALIFORNIA, HARBOUR ISLAND_THE BAHAMAS NEW YORK_NEW YORK, LON
IAMI BEACH_FLORIDA, NANTUCKET_MASSACHUSETTS MIAMI BEACH_FLORIDA PALM
EACH_FLORIDA, MORRIS_CONNECTICUT BOSTON_MASSACHUSETTS, PORTLAND_ORE
IAMI BEACH_FLORIDA DOLORES_COLORADO SANTA BARBARA_CALIFORNIA, PORTLAN
EW YORK_NEW YORK, HARBOUR ISLAND_THE BAHAMAS, MIAMI BEACH_FLORIDA, LO
LAND_NEW YORK ISLAMORADA_FLORIDA, SARANAC LAKE_NEW YORK, MIAMI BEACH
RINGS_CALIFORNIA, NANTUCKET_MASSACHUSETTS PALM SPRINGS_CALIFORNIA, L
EATTLE_WASHINGTON KEY WEST_FLORIDA, JACKSON_WYOMING ISLAMORADA_FLOR
ORTLAND_OREGON, MIAMI BEACH_FLORIDA, LITTLE TORCH KEY_FLORIDA, MIAMI
EACH_FLORIDA, LOS ANGELES_CALIFORNIA, PALM SPRINGS_CALIFORNIA, HARBOU
ORK, MIAMI BEACH_FLORIDA GREENOUGH_MONTANA, MIAMI BEACH_FLORIDA, NAN
RINGS_CALIFORNIA, LOS ANGELES_CALIFORNIA MIAMI BEACH_FLORIDA, MORRIS_
CKSON_WYOMING ISLAMORADA_FLORIDA, NEW YORK_NEW YORK, MIAMI BEACH_FL
EY_FLORIDA, MIAMI BEACH_FLORIDA, PALM SPRINGS_CALIFORNIA NEW YORK_NE
RINGS_CALIFORNIA, HARBOUR ISLAND_THE BAHAMAS NEW YORK_NEW YORK

REMOTE REFUGES

- Architecture/Design: Luxury lodge
- Highlight: The alpine pool
- To pack: Ski or fishing gear—you won't be spending long in the hotel

AMANGANI

Jackson Hole, Wyoming

The Aman brand is revered among travelers and the design set alike. The Singapore-based company famous for its visionary hotels—most of which feature a hefty quotient of luxury—has been wowing the media, aesthetes, and serious jetsetters for more than two decades thanks to increasingly innovative and extraordinary architecture and increasingly innovative and impressive destinations. Most of these destinations are located in Asia, where Aman's streamlined designs seem to perfectly suit the Asian landscapes and penchant for understated style. And so, when Aman decided to decamp to Jackson Hole, Wyoming, right in the middle of the Wild West, and build an amazing resort against the imposing Grand Tetons, the move caused a few heads to turn. After all, the landscape had always been more suited to rustic than streamlined luxury. What was Aman going to do? Build a cowboy ranch? No, said Aman's architects, headed by the famously talented Edward Tuttle, we're going to stick with what we do best, which is out-and-out luxury, but we're going to use the Tetons as inspiration. The result is mountain architecture at its most beautiful.

Amangani rises up from the hillside of Gros Ventre Butte like a grand, man-made peak, with its rough Oklahoma-sandstone walls arching up gracefully in the shape of a mountainside. Overlooking the valley of Jackson Hole and the Snake River Range without dominating them, the resort's materials—stone and Pacific redwood—are not only suited to the area but reflect the same coloring of the rich browns of the mountains in summer. And the pool—a sophisticated, 100-foot sliver of silvery water—reflects the wide skies and clouds like a magnificent outdoor mirror.

Inside, the hotel is more understated but no less glamorous. The hotel seems less opulent than most five-star establishments but at the same time feels more luxurious. And it's the craftsmanship that does it. There are magnificent fireplaces, slate-walled bathrooms, redwood floors, indulgent soaking tubs, and of course ample balconies to take in that view. Some of the interior spaces are on the minimalist side, but it's only to draw the focus back to the mountains. It is a place with integrity, a place that realizes that the real drawcard here is the landscape: the dramatic, classic American Wild West. And while the architecture isn't rustic or ranch-like, it still feels right for this site, as though it has been here almost as long as the Tetons.

This part of America first came to prominence when John D. Rockefeller, Jr., who fell in love with the region while traveling through it in the 1920s, decided to preserve much of the area by buying up huge tracts of land. In doing so, he protected it from development and laid the foundations for what eventually became the 310,000-acre Grand Teton National Park. Today, Grand Teton Country's 3.5 million acres is still 97 percent protected by National Forests, National Parks, and wildlife preserves. Thanks to this preservation, the mountains are still king here; the air is still crisp and the roads and mountain paths still relatively quiet. Even though Jackson Hole is one of the best places to ski in North America, the atmosphere is down-to-earth rather than flashy. Celebrities such as Harrison Ford may own properties here, but they come here for the scenery rather than to be seen.

Amangani shares the same philosophy. It has put the focus back on the environment rather than on the architecture. Its clean, simple lines are designed to stand out, but at the same time bow down in respect to the grander lines of the mountain ranges around it.

Photography courtesy Aman Hotels & Resorts

- Architecture/Design: Glamping it up—glamour camping in style
- Highlight: The scenery
- To pack: Good boots, for riding or hiking

THE RESORT AT PAWS UP
Greenough, Montana

Set in Montana's majestic Big Sky country, this hideaway is part of the new "glamping" trend sweeping the globe. Think of the luxury safari tents that were first set up in Africa, India, and the Australian Outback with enormous success. Well, now the idea has been transplanted to Montana at a former cattle ranch set in the Blackfoot Valley, 3,800 feet above sea level. It's a brilliant move because out here you're compelled to commune with nature, to experience the pristine setting first-hand, and there's no better way to do it than by peeking through a canvas flap.

The Resort at Paws Up offers six safari-style tents and six similar riverside tents equipped with king-size feather beds, Native American rugs, and full electricity, so you can enjoy urban luxuries while still feeling at one with nature. The riverside tents are set right on the water, so you can experience the pleasure of falling asleep while listening to the river wind its way past. There's artwork on the canvas walls, huge private timber decks with table and chairs, a cute hat stand upon which to throw your Stetson, and even a "camping butler" to fix you dinner. As Paws Up wittily offers, roughing it has never been so refined.

The resort also features 28 guest houses, ranging from the so-called Big Timber Homes to a farmhouse, a bunkhouse, meadow homes, and a Blackfoot River lodge, so you can sneak into a proper dwelling with real walls when the great outdoors becomes all too much. Decked out with features such as stone fireplaces and outdoor hot tubs, and enhanced further with animal-skin rugs and cowboy portraits, it's a place that firmly embraces the Montana aesthetic with no apologies whatsoever.

Paws Up explains that this destination is designed for people who want to rough it without really roughing it, and there seems to be a lot of them because the resort is constantly booked out. It's interesting that while numbers to North American national parks are declining, visitors to these kinds of glamping destinations are on the rise. Perhaps it's the soft adventure that appeals—no hassles, no having to put up the tents, no cooking, no fighting over the last section of the blown-up mattress—just nature and nurture. No wonder people are forking out big money for the experience.

Photography courtesy The Resort at Paws Up

DUNTON HOT SPRINGS

Dolores, Colorado

There have been some truly extraordinary hotels fashioned out of some truly extraordinary shells, but until the Dunton Hot Springs came along, none had ever been created out of a ghost town. The captivating collection of log buildings that has become one of North America's most distinctive destinations sits at an altitude of 8,600 feet on the west fork of the Dolores River in the San Juan Mountains in Colorado, halfway between the ski town of Telluride and the Anasazi ruins of Mesa Verde. It is remote mountain country, almost inaccessible in winter, but like most things remote it is well worth the journey. The majestic landscape of the Colorado Rockies serves as a reminder that you are far from urban life, but it is only after seeing the beautifully restored, hand-hewn, century-old log cabins of the formerly abandoned gold prospectors' camp that you realize you're well and truly in a different world.

Dunton began life in 1885 as a camp for the nearby Emma mine. Later, when locals discovered there were hot springs here—the perfect way to wash off the grime from a hard day's work—they wholeheartedly embraced this new distraction. The savvy Roscio family, who had bought the land on which the hot springs were located, not only decided to charge a nickel for the bathing but also opened a lodge, bar, and built more cabins for the miners. The first hot tub was created by simply digging a pit, lining it with logs, and diverting the hot water to fill the hole. It was so successful that the design has changed little since. The remoteness of the area, however, along with the end of the mining boom, made life unbearably tough and eventually Dunton fell into disrepair.

Then in 1994 Christoph Henkel passed through the region in search of property in Telluride. He saw Dunton, fell in love with its atmosphere and its dilapidated cabins with their stove-pipe chimneys, and bought it on the spot. Originally, Henkel intended to keep it as a retreat for his family, but eventually decided to open property to the public as a unique rustic hideaway for those wanting to experience life as it was in the days of the Wild West. Henkel added to the motley collection of cabins by driving around and making offers for other authentic old buildings. He then added further authentic details, such as porches with boot scrapers and boxes for spare firewood, and slowly restored the camp, shack by shack, until the character of Dunton emerged again.

Now it's as if the miners had never left—there's even a dance hall, a church, and a saloon. You don't need to blink to imagine you're back in the days of gun-draws and bar-room brawls, but if you're under the impression it's more rustic and less luxury, think again. Christoph's wife, Katrin Henkel, is an Old Masters specialist as well as being co-owner of Colnaghi, in London's Bond Street. She is also an interior designer and has outfitted the cabins in beautiful detail. Directors chairs hang from ceilings in an ornate style, luxurious beds are dressed in high-count white linens, bathrooms feature thick towels and Elemis toiletries, porches are outfitted with wicker-loom chairs and elegant rugs, lamps, wagon-wheel chandeliers, and a variety of other American-southwest antiques adorn the atmospheric timber spaces. There is a library cabin with books on ghost towns and the Wild West and a fireplace to read them by. And there is the famous saloon, a place where, legend has it, Butch Cassidy and the Sundance Kid hid out after robbing the Telluride bank.

The highlight, however, is the hot springs. And there is a choice of how you can get wet at Dunton. You can choose to immerse yourself in the Well House cabin, indulge in the restored 19th-century bathhouse, plunge into one of the pools, dip your toes in at the source, or simply wade into the river at Christoph's Spring. Then, when you're so relaxed you can't feel your toes, you can stagger out, dress, and whet your appetite with Dunton's impressive wine and food menu.

The Henkels have designed Dunton Hot Springs to be a destination of contradictions: the old blends with the new and the rustic log cabins and life-worn saloon present an authentic backdrop for a week of pure pampering. Out here, the architecture, the snow-capped mountains, the river, the wide skies, and the haunting beauty of Monument Valley are considered as luxurious as the heli-skiing, the fine wines, the organic food, and the service. As Christoph Henkel says, "Luxury is space and time." Dunton Hot Springs truly is one of America's most remarkable retreats: a place that takes you back to the past while reminding you how good the present is. No wonder most of the guests are repeat visitors.

Photography courtesy Dunton Hot Springs

- Architecture/Design: Rustic splendor
- Highlight: The lake and mountain views
- To pack: Nothing—this place has everything you need to relax

THE POINT

New York, New York

The Point needs little introduction for weary, wealthy professionals seeking refuge from the rigors of Manhattan. Built in the Great Camp style, this legendary retreat has been a haven for decades and over the years has established a reputation for cosseting of the most incredible kind. It's like a private, lakefront estate owned by an affluent friend who's decided to hold an exclusive house party—a lavish, splendid, potentially memorable one—and has thought to invite you. The anticipation bubbles up before you even reach the front gate.

The essence of The Point is seclusion. Hidden away on Saranac Lake, in the heart of the Adirondacks in upstate New York, it has a Great Camp philosophy that discourages phones or televisions, gently suggesting that if you wanted to work you would have stayed in New York. The Point has relaxation down to a fine art—it's the kind of place that manages to be both wonderfully luxurious and down-to-earth, both unpretentious and splendid, in the one fabulous and inspirational package.

For those from outside North America who have never heard of Great Camps or their distinctive style, these wilderness retreats were first commissioned by families such as the Vanderbilts, the Morgans, the Astors, and the Carnegies who wanted to escape New York and Boston for the countryside. But, of course, these families wanted simplicity without the simplicity, so, as the wealthy tend to do, they redefined the word. They built their camps but they built them in a "great" style—actually an extravagant one. Most Great Camps were—and still are—mini compounds of luxury, small villages unto themselves with extensive and lavish accommodations for the family, grand lodges for the main guests, additional staff quarters for the servants, and plush boat houses and garages to house both wooden boats and expensive vehicles. It seems the ultra rich had a grander idea of simplicity than the rest of us.

The Point originally belonged to William Avery Rockefeller and has all the standard features you'd find in a Great Camp, including a Great Hall where guests dine and lavish cabins on the lake to retreat to afterwards. There are 11 guest quarters spread among four original buildings, so the setting is intimate while still being private and spacious. Each room has lake views, a custom-made bed, a sitting area in front of an enormous stone fireplace, and a mixture of antiques and Adirondack furniture. These are rooms that encourage reflection out over the water and up toward the mountains. The Adirondack wilderness is beloved for its lakes, streams, and timberlands, and The Point has been positioned perfectly to take in this famous landscape.

But The Point also has that something extra—that X factor that some hoteliers and developers manage to pinpoint without seemingly trying at all. This is a destination that feels more like a home than a hotel or retreat. The furniture is fashioned from timber or logs, the walls are broad timber slabs with cathedral ceilings, the stone fireplaces are always lit, and somehow the hunting trophies and mounted moose heads don't appear that scary. There is an authentic rustic splendor about this establishment.

While the architecture and rooms are akin to the turn-of-the-century Great Camps, the food is determinedly contemporary. World-renowned, three-Michelin-star, London-based chef Albert Roux has trained all the chefs here and the meals are certainly a reflection of their dedication and talent. Dining in the 30- by 50-foot Great Hall in The Main Lodge is an experience in itself, but when the platters come out The Point really shows what it can do.

There is only one catch to this place, and of course it's the cost. The Point is among the most expensive places to stay in America and rates must be paid in advance. What this does mean, however, is that once you arrive you can really feel as though you're thoroughly looked after, with nothing left to pay. All you need to do is take some of the very fine wine and a picnic basket out on one of The Point's beautifully made mahogany boats and pretend you're a Rockefeller, back in the days when simplicity looked like this.

Photography courtesy The Point

- Architecture/Design: Tent chic
- Highlight: The walking tracks to the sea
- To pack: Comfortable walking shoes

EL CAPITAN CANYON

Santa Barbara, California

Only in America could a place like El Capitan Canyon have been conceived. Based on the American fondness for camping, El Capitan Canyon has been described as a "rich man's campground," because here everything's been done for you. All you need to do is loosen the tent flap and pull up the duvet. This destination is designed for those who love the idea of camping but wouldn't know a tent peg if they tripped over one.

Nestled in historic groves of oak and sycamore trees along El Capitan Creek, a 10-minute walk from the beautifully wild, unspoiled stretch of California known as El Capitan State Beach, the campground is a site for sore urban eyes. For a start, "campground" is a bit of an understatement—it's more of a luxury hideaway. And "tents" don't really do these dwellings justice either—most of them have more creature comforts than our own homes. The collections of cedar cabins and luxury safari tents are grouped in villages with evocative names—Stone Pine, Peace Tree, Lone Stone, and Shaded Creek. Once you find your village, you find your cabin or tent for the night, although each is set far apart from the others to offer a measure of privacy and is surrounded by the leafy branches of giant sycamores to give the effect of really being in the wild.

The rustic scene belies the luxury inside each of these dwellings, which often comes as a surprise for those expecting a camp bed and an enamel washbasin. Each of the luxury safari tents, or "canvas chalets" as they are sometimes called, measures 12 by 14 feet and is set upon a raised, wide, wooden platform. All tents have screened windows and zip-down flaps, and are furnished with ornate willow beds (complete with linens, duvets, and Wild West-inspired blankets), bedside tables, chairs, a small desk, a storage trunk, and coat hooks. There's also a small heater and electric lamps for lighting, and outside there is a private fire pit and picnic table—perfect for fireside gatherings at night. The cozy cedar cabins are even plusher, with kitchenettes, full bathrooms, hardwood floors, and bed linens that belong at a fancy hotel. Some even have Jacuzzi tubs and many come with lofts accessible by ladders, which kids tend to love. As do adults, for that matter.

El Capital Canyon says that its "camp is designed to be an antidote to all that is excessive, formal, artificial, or contrived." The estate wants to retain the unspoiled nature of the environment while offering guests a different way of experiencing it. It's pampering with the pleasures of the wild right outside, and it's also surprisingly serene. Guests love nothing more than sitting out on their deck listening to the frogs and watching the monarch butterflies or walking down to the beach for a swim or stroll along the shore. By the end of their day, most have usually forgotten the hassle of LA freeways, the stress of work, or the weight of their mortgages. El Capitan Canyon takes them to another place—physically and emotionally.

The only problem with this place is that it's so relaxing that you never want to go back to ordinary camping again. El Capitan Canyon, I fear, has spoiled it for all of us.

Photography courtesy Steven Lam

• Architecture/Design: Experimental and extraordinary
• Highlight: The Helicopter Suite
• To pack: A camera and many rolls of film

WINVIAN

Morris, Connecticut

If you've ever wanted to sleep in a helicopter, a library, or a hunter's lodge, then Winvian is the destination for you. There's just one word to describe this place: eccentric. Okay, perhaps two: eccentric and extraordinary. Forbes.com, the online version of the magazine, included Winvian in a list of the world's great unconventional hotels. Although more conventional than the Ice Hotel in Canada and the Undersea Lodge in Key Large, it still packs a hefty design punch. If you're fortunate enough to visit Winvian then prepare to be surprised—in so many ways.

Tucked away in the landed old-money hills of Connecticut, Winvian is like a punk rocker who has wandered into a party of blue bloods. Developed by the Smith family, the resort has been designed to cater to cashed-up eco-boomers and wealthy travelers looking for something different, a special destination that they can boast about to their friends back home.

To start with there are the rooms, if you can use such a prosaic word. The Helicopter cottage features a hulking, 17,000-pound Sikorsky HH37 Sea King Pelican chopper, rotors and all, although it has been renovated so it now features a wet bar rather than compartments to store rescue equipment. The Golf cottage, on the other hand, has gently sloping floors, so you can putt from your bed to your own private outside green. And the Treehouse is set— you guessed it—35 feet above ground, although you'll be reassured to hear that its wood-burning fireplaces are set in rubber so they don't sway like the rest of the building. There is also the Library; the Beaver Lodge, complete with an authentic, log-tangled, beaver den preserved above the bed; the Secret Society, a Masonic-style temple; Maritime, a lighthouse in the woods; and Stone, the most luxurious cave you'll ever sleep in.

The fifteen architects that were commissioned to design the eighteen cottages were obviously given a wide berth to design something truly outlandish, because the result is a glorious architectural idiosyncrasy of the most memorable kind. Other features include complimentary hot-air balloon rides, a 5,000-square-foot private spa, and bikes at each cottage for transport. Winvian is an experience rather than a mere hotel or destination. The resort's cheeky slogan is "hold your hat," which is certainly appropriate—you never know what's going to happen here. It's a flight of fancy, but it's also very, very fun.

Interior photography courtesy Miki Ouisterhof; Exterior photography courtesy Winvian

HAMAS, MIAMI BEACH_FLORIDA, LOS ANGELES_CALIFORNIA, PALM SPRINGS_CALI
RANAC LAKE_NEW YORK, MIAMI BEACH_FLORIDA GREENOUGH_MONTANA, MIAMI B
NTUCKET_MASSACHUSETTS PALM SPRINGS_CALIFORNIA, LOS ANGELES_CALIFORNIA
ATTLE_WASHINGTON KEY WEST_FLORIDA, JACKSON_WYOMING ISLAMORADA_FLORI
RTLAND_OREGON, MIAMI BEACH_FLORIDA, LITTLE TORCH KEY_FLORIDA, MIAMI B
ACH_FLORIDA, LOS ANGELES_CALIFORNIA, PALM SPRINGS_CALIFORNIA, HARBOUR
ORK, MIAMI BEACH_FLORIDA GREENOUGH_MONTANA, MIAMI BEACH_FLORIDA, NAN
RINGS_CALIFORNIA, LOS ANGELES_CALIFORNIA MIAMI BEACH_FLORIDA, MORRIS_C
CKSON_WYOMING ISLAMORADA_FLORIDA, NEW YORK_NEW YORK, MIAMI BEACH_FL
Y_FLORIDA, MIAMI BEACH_FLORIDA, PALM SPRINGS_CALIFORNIA NEW YORK_NEW
RINGS_CALIFORNIA, HARBOUR ISLAND_THE BAHAMAS NEW YORK_NEW YORK, LON
AMI BEACH_FLORIDA, NANTUCKET_MASSACHUSETTS MIAMI BEACH_FLORIDA PALM
ACH_FLORIDA, MORRIS_CONNECTICUT BOSTON_MASSACHUSETTS, PORTLAND_ORE
AMI BEACH_FLORIDA DOLORES_COLORADO SANTA BARBARA_CALIFORNIA, PORTLAN
W YORK_NEW YORK, HARBOUR ISLAND_THE BAHAMAS, MIAMI BEACH_FLORIDA, LO
LAND_NEW YORK ISLAMORADA_FLORIDA, SARANAC LAKE_NEW YORK MIAMI BEACH
RINGS_CALIFORNIA, NANTUCKET_MASSACHUSETTS PALM SPRINGS_CALIFORNIA, LO
ATTLE_WASHINGTON KEY WEST_FLORIDA, JACKSON_WYOMING ISLAMORADA_FLORI
RTLAND_OREGON, MIAMI BEACH_FLORIDA, LITTLE TORCH KEY_FLORIDA, MIAMI B
ACH_FLORIDA, LOS ANGELES_CALIFORNIA, PALM SPRINGS_CALIFORNIA, HARBOUR
ORK, MIAMI BEACH_FLORIDA GREENOUGH_MONTANA, MIAMI BEACH_FLORIDA, NAN
RINGS_CALIFORNIA, LOS ANGELES_CALIFORNIA MIAMI BEACH_FLORIDA, MORRIS_C
CKSON_WYOMING ISLAMORADA_FLORIDA, NEW YORK_NEW YORK, MIAMI BEACH_FL
Y_FLORIDA, MIAMI BEACH_FLORIDA, PALM SPRINGS_CALIFORNIA NEW YORK_NEW
RINGS_CALIFORNIA, HARBOUR ISLAND_THE BAHAMAS NEW YORK_NEW YORK, LON
AMI BEACH_FLORIDA, NANTUCKET_MASSACHUSETTS MIAMI BEACH_FLORIDA PALM
ACH_FLORIDA, MORRIS_CONNECTICUT BOSTON_MASSACHUSETTS, PORTLAND_ORE
AMI BEACH_FLORIDA DOLORES_COLORADO SANTA BARBARA_CALIFORNIA, PORTLAN
W YORK_NEW YORK, HARBOUR ISLAND_THE BAHAMAS, MIAMI BEACH_FLORIDA, LO
LAND_NEW YORK ISLAMORADA_FLORIDA, SARANAC LAKE_NEW YORK, MIAMI BEACH
RINGS_CALIFORNIA, NANTUCKET_MASSACHUSETTS PALM SPRINGS_CALIFORNIA, LO
ATTLE_WASHINGTON KEY WEST_FLORIDA, JACKSON_WYOMING ISLAMORADA_FLORI
RTLAND_OREGON, MIAMI BEACH_FLORIDA, LITTLE TORCH KEY_FLORIDA, MIAMI B
ACH_FLORIDA, LOS ANGELES_CALIFORNIA, PALM SPRINGS_CALIFORNIA, HARBOUR
ORK, MIAMI BEACH_FLORIDA GREENOUGH_MONTANA, MIAMI BEACH_FLORIDA, NAN
RINGS_CALIFORNIA, LOS ANGELES_CALIFORNIA MIAMI BEACH_FLORIDA, MORRIS_C
CKSON_WYOMING ISLAMORADA_FLORIDA, NEW YORK_NEW YORK, MIAMI BEACH_FL
Y_FLORIDA, MIAMI BEACH_FLORIDA, PALM SPRINGS_CALIFORNIA NEW YORK_NEW
RINGS_CALIFORNIA, HARBOUR ISLAND_THE BAHAMAS NEW YORK_NEW YORK, LON
AMI BEACH_FLORIDA, NANTUCKET_MASSACHUSETTS MIAMI BEACH_FLORIDA PALM
ACH_FLORIDA, MORRIS_CONNECTICUT BOSTON_MASSACHUSETTS, PORTLAND_ORE
AMI BEACH_FLORIDA DOLORES_COLORADO SANTA BARBARA_CALIFORNIA, PORTLAN
W YORK_NEW YORK, HARBOUR ISLAND_THE BAHAMAS, MIAMI BEACH_FLORIDA, LO
LAND_NEW YORK ISLAMORADA_FLORIDA, SARANAC LAKE_NEW YORK, MIAMI BEACH
RINGS_CALIFORNIA, NANTUCKET_MASSACHUSETTS PALM SPRINGS_CALIFORNIA, LO
ATTLE_WASHINGTON KEY WEST_FLORIDA, JACKSON_WYOMING ISLAMORADA_FLORI
RTLAND_OREGON, MIAMI BEACH_FLORIDA, LITTLE TORCH KEY_FLORIDA, MIAMI
ACH_FLORIDA, LOS ANGELES_CALIFORNIA, PALM SPRINGS_CALIFORNIA, HARBOUR
ORK, MIAMI BEACH_FLORIDA GREENOUGH_MONTANA, MIAMI BEACH_FLORIDA, NAN
RINGS_CALIFORNIA, LOS ANGELES_CALIFORNIA MIAMI BEACH_FLORIDA, MORRIS_
CKSON_WYOMING ISLAMORADA_FLORIDA, NEW YORK_NEW YORK, MIAMI BEACH_F
Y_FLORIDA, MIAMI BEACH_FLORIDA, PALM SPRINGS_CALIFORNIA NEW YORK_NEW
RINGS_CALIFORNIA, HARBOUR ISLAND_THE BAHAMAS NEW YORK_NEW YORK, LON

CHIC HIDEAWAYS

- Architecture/Design: Trim and taut—just like its guests
- Highlight: Proximity to Rodeo Drive
- To pack: Your designer sunglasses and a spare credit card for the shopping

THE CRESCENT

Beverly Hills, California

The Crescent in Beverly Hills is a little like many of the actresses in LA: petite and perfectly formed, with barely a wrinkle or crease in sight. It's fashionably lithe but full of style and personality, and fond of privacy while still being ultra-glamorous and excited by any attention it gets. And while its public areas are crisply chic and properly attired, its private rooms feature mini bars that are imbued with wicked humor, Intimacy Kits and all. All in all, The Crescent is cheeky, chic, and full of character: just as the perfect LA hotel should be.

Built as a place to house movie stars of the silent firm era, The Crescent was badly in need of a Hollywood facelift when it was bought and refurbished by Gregory Peck and The Crescent Hotel Group in 2001. The location was perfect and the hotel's structure was still in good condition, but both the façade and interior badly needed an overhaul. Enter designer Dodd Mitchell.

Out went the dour exterior and uninspiring floor plan and in came the shimmeringly beautiful white dining room, the coolly glamorous foyer, the startlingly ingenious terrace and its indoor–outdoor fireplace, the breezy alfresco restaurant, and the elegant new "face," with its twin palm trees and front door that wittily says Lounge and Sleep—although it should say Party, Drink, and Be Gorgeous somewhere on the glass too. Now, after settling into its new changes, the hotel is a clever mix of private club-style atmosphere and LA fab. In short, the place is very cool.

The thing is, you won't find the normal accoutrements of LA's hotels here. There are no blue Astroturf bits, no shag-carpet ceilings, no sniffy staff doing time while waiting for their big break, no roped-off areas for guests only, and no odd courtesy bikinis that dissolve in water. Indeed, there are almost no over-the-top architectural or interior design features at all. If you want design thrills, best go to an André Balazs hotel. At The Crescent there is only calm and style.

crescent

LOUNGE   SLEEP

The most innovative areas of The Crescent are the public spaces. Each is a fusion of functionality, form, and style. The breakfast terrace, complete with nougat-colored, daybed-style seating and bolster cushions, doubles as a peaceful place to read during the day before turning into a fireplace-enhanced cocktail lounge in the evening. It also blends seamlessly with the outdoor restaurant, called Boé, which is an extension of the funky bar. The white foyer is equally inviting and features low-slung sofas to lounge around on while you're waiting for friends to meet you for drinks.

The downside of The Crescent is that, although it's private it is also boutique-sized, meaning that the standard rooms can be smaller than you might expect. If you like your personal space on the luxurious side, it may be best to upgrade your room. The bathroom walls have been redesigned in a glossy, concrete-style rendering that feels very industrial and modern, but the monastic gray color offers visual relief from the acres of black and white. Also standard are luxurious toiletries and robes to really make you feel like a movie star. All rooms feature flatscreen TVs, low-slung platform beds with beautiful Italian linen and eiderdowns, in-built iPods with the hotel's carefully selected menu of songs, and courtesy magazines such as Vanity Fair. The rooms may be intimate, but they're packed with pleasures. And really, you're not in LA to lie around in bed anyway—you'll be down at Rodeo Drive or clubbing/caffeining/shopping in West Hollywood for most of your stay.

A prime example of the glamorous new hideaways that are popping up all over the US, the Crescent and its owners are indicative of the growing market of hotels and hoteliers catering for a new generation of guests who want style over hype. After the explosion of designer hotels in the past few years, people are now wary of over-designed spaces. Guests want inspiration and innovation but they also want relaxation—a destination to retreat to after a frazzled day of business meetings or touring the local sights. And you can't relax when your hotel is so funky that you can't work out how to use the bathroom door. Nor is it much fun when there's a glass window between the bath and bed, making privacy a thing of dreams.

Gregory Peck argues that his hotel is more of a unique hotel than a boutique hotel: it's designed more for the quiet aesthete than the voyeur looking for a thrill. His hotels are not attention-grabbers actively looking for publicity and headlines, but rather are classic beauties styled after hotels of a bygone era, such as Claridge's of London or the George V in Paris. Press materials for The Crescent and its sister properties talk of a "unique aesthetic" drawn "from the past era when travel by rail, ship, and airplane was considered the pinnacle of luxury." Peck, just like his Hollywood namesake, hopes to reflect a classic elegance and vitality.

Sleek, cheeky, and full of grace and good humor, The Crescent is very much like the best Hollywood stars, only without the diva attitude. You can't help but adore it. If only they handed out Oscars for hotel design.

Photography courtesy The Crescent

■ Architecture/Design: Distinguished, old-school
■ Highlight: The black-and-white foyer
■ To pack: Stress—it's a place that seriously pampers

XV BEACON

Boston, Massachusetts

The Fifteen Beacon (shown in its branding as XV Beacon) is quintessentially Boston. The traditional, sophisticated, determinedly monochromatic color palette is the same one favored by the city's top lawyers and business people (lots of grays, blacks, mocha-browns, whites, and smart checks), and the design, right down to the name, is grand and dignified but Spartan too—very New England. And just as the famous Massachusetts city is noted for its somber ways, so too is the Beacon a keystone of civility and seriousness.

Refurbished from an original Beaux Arts building located in a prestigious, blue-blood part of town, right near Boston Common, the hotel was outfitted by Paul Roiff, a specialist in renovating Boston buildings, in a style designed to attract a certain set—the upmarket, sophisticated, discerning set. But the refit was so successful that the place has become known right through North America, and now everyone from fashion models to families checks in for some proper Boston pampering.

The statement exterior, with its swags and gilded shields, and the dramatic black-and-white lobby with its high-backed white chairs, black lacquer walls, and black-and-white checked floor, sets the tone from the start. It's the sort of space that says old-world elegance and exclusivity without having any discernable snob quality layered over the top. While the rooms give off a gentlemanly vibe, the subtle design stops them from arching too far toward the wealthy bachelor pad look. The fireplaces (each room has one) are done in floating stainless steel, some of the beds are four-poster, the walls lined in dark wood, and the tables dressed with two-foot-tall candlesticks. There are also marble busts and museum-quality artwork to give that sense of Boston history and lots of dark mahogany to add that old-fashioned Yankee feel. There are some quirky touches—for example, the cage elevator is paneled in red leather—but these, too, are marked by style and understatement.

It's a hotel loved by business travelers because there are three telephones in every room, a flatscreen TV in bathrooms to keep an eye on the stock markets, an in-room safe that also allows you to recharge your laptop, and a car service with a Lexus and driver at guests' disposal. And it's also short distance from the city's financial district. The hotel also offers surprising little indulgences, including bathrooms stocked with heavenly toiletries to polish away even the deepest stress fractures, from buckwheat eye pillows to peppermint foot lotions, vegetable oil soaps, and aromatherapy jet lag packages.

Luxurious and dignified without being stuffy or buttoned up, the Beacon has remained true to its name in terms of good taste ever since it opened in 2000. It has never put a foot wrong and in fact goes to great lengths to do the right thing by its guests. You could almost move in here permanently and do business from your bathtub, such is the technology incorporated into this place. Well, who wouldn't feel at home with a fireplace, heated towel racks, Italian linen, half bottles of Château Lafite Rothschild and Krug Champagne. Fresh toiletries, and a minibar filled with treats. It's a wonder half of Boston isn't here, hanging out and being pampered while they do business. Oh, wait a minute—they are!

Photography courtesy Dom Miguel and XV Beacon

THE HORIZON HOTEL

Palm Springs, California

There is something about Palm Springs—the desert, the mountains, the climate, the sunshine, the mirage-like element—that inspires extraordinary architecture, and notable architects have been retreating here for more than half a century to design remarkable dwellings. Not surprisingly, many of these astonishing projects are still standing, homages to fine lines and desert pleasures. One of these sun-kissed treasures is The Horizon Hotel, a beautiful hideaway that's starting to attract a legion of design fans seeking to immerse themselves in the town's mid-century magic.

Built in 1952 by architect William Cody as a retreat for Hollywood mogul Jack Wrather and his wife, The Horizon originally started life as a house, called L'Horizon. Wrather already had several properties, including a Holmby Hills mansion in Los Angeles, a townhouse in London, and several other residences, but he wanted a Palm Springs haven; a place to which he could retreat to do business and then do pleasure, together with a posse of his closest family and friends.

Wrather had plenty of money, having made his fortune as a movie and television producer (*The Lone Ranger*, *Lassie*) and also through ownership of a yachting company, The Disneyland Hotel, the Queen Mary, and Howard Hughes's wooden airplane, the Spruce Goose, but he didn't necessarily want a grand estate. What he did want was something distinct, something that suited the Palm Springs lifestyle and climate. So, he asked architect William Cody to design a subtle and inconspicuous, yet still sophisticated, compound. Cody came up with L'Horizon, a sleek, low-slung estate featuring a principal three-bedroom residence surrounded by glass-walled bungalows, all set around a large pool on two and a half manicured acres. Most of the rooms faced the mountain views, with the glass designed to provide uninterrupted views out to the landscape and sky. It cost $250,000 and it was one of Cody's best designs. L'Horizon would also become the scene for the Wrather's notable gatherings for more than three decades—until Palm Springs's decline, when most of the good and great moved on.

Fast forward to 2004 and a developer called Dave Scharf. who saw the promise of this once-loved home and, together with former Cody associate Frank Urrutia, embarked on a plan to restore the property and return it to its former glory. He renamed it The Horizon Hotel and opened it as a retreat for architecture lovers. The restoration was so successful that Cody's daughter gave it her tick of approval, saying her father would have been pleased. It had, she said, retained its spirit.

The Horizon Hotel does indeed have a spirit. Whether it's Cody's, Wrather's, or simply those of guests past, there is a special feeling here. It's not simply a place people come to escape LA, stick on their sunglasses, and recline by the pool in privacy. It's an oasis, just as Cody intended it to be. It may be the fact that it was once a private home, but there is an intimacy here, a laid-back elegance that encourages guests to linger, to chat with each other, to talk about their lives over cocktails by the pool.

The design is still recognized as the mid-century modern style and all the features designed by Cody have been retained. The lines are clean, the façade simple. Rooms flow from inside to out via a monochromatic palette and the minimal black-on-white décor even continues through to the pool bar. It is a graceful space: well designed, well dressed, and ever-so-pleasing to the eye. For some reason the lack of clutter feels comfortable. Cody knew what he was doing all right: a century after it was built, L'Horizon is still an oasis on the horizon.

Photography courtesy The Horizon Hotel

MONDRIAN

South Beach, Florida

Mondrian in Miami had a lot to live up to. Its predecessor, Mondrian in Los Angeles, broke all the rules of design when it first opened and consequently graced the pages of just about every design magazine or newspaper supplement in North America and indeed around the world. Designed by Philippe Starck and featuring a nightclub, Skybar, by Rande Gerber, it was so glamorous it was immediately adopted as the home-away-from-home for Hollywood's celebrities and fashionistas seeking a place to escape to—and play up—in private. Most of them must have wished that there was also a Mondrian for when they were working or worshipping the sun down in the famous Floridian city. Well, now Mondrian Miami has answered their calls. And yes, it's as gorgeous, as glamorous, and as architecturally witty as its LA cousin.

Designed by Marcel Wanders, South Beach's Mondrian is hotel design at its most daring. It was a stroke of genius to hire Wanders, who made his name as a designer for the likes of B&B Italia, Poliform, Moroso, Flos, and Moooi, although it was also a risky move, as his designs often veer toward the unexpected. In this instance the risk has paid off—Mondrian is a masterpiece.

According to Wanders, Mondrian was inspired by Sleeping Beauty's castle and comprises a series of highly theatrical, witty spaces that flow from one to the other in a fantastic story of design, form, line, and style. There are oversized white columns that look like the giant contoured legs of tables, black 'Smoke' chairs that form silhouettes against a background of stark white walls, giant gold bells inlaid with glittering chandeliers, neo-baroque furniture, and a shimmering white floor that's made for dancing. The mostly white foyer is only punctuated by a swooping, jet-black, laser-cut steel staircase that spirals like a grand staircase in a fairytale castle to the upper mezzanine level. It's more of a dramatic signature showpiece for the hotel than an ordinary staircase.

In the Sunset Lounge, the magic continues with charmingly etched, tinted mirrors, more candelabras, onyx, jewel-cut stools scattered between ottomans, and gold-leaf wallpaper that beautifully offsets a dark herringboned floor. The most surprising part of the hotel though is the pool area, a fanciful, exuberant space full of wonderful corners. There are gigantic grassy cabanas, formed from topiaried hedges and trained into an arc, that are fitted out with couches and flatscreen TVs, splash-proof red rubber faux-Louis chairs posing cheekily under enormous, oversized tented areas draped with billowy white curtains, sandpits with bouncy toys, and lush, labyrinthine gardens with their own secret "kissing gardens" enclosed within.

It's all very *Sleeping Beauty*, albeit for the 21st century. And, just like the original fairytale, everyone seems to love it. The hotel's motif—a giant doll's head—is meant to represent Sleeping Beauty herself, although it's more funky Miami Beauty and less Brothers Grimm. Mondrian was designed to be a fantasy, and it's certainly that. It's a flirtatious wink at architecture rather than a solemn ode to it. Nothing is what it seems, and that's what Wanders intended. Even the showerheads are styled as crystal chandeliers and the vanities are edgy horizontal platforms of granite encased in glass.

Mondrian has also set out to answer all your desires and if you've forgotten anything, even the Bentley, you can buy what you need in a wall-sized vending machine, which does away with the old-fashioned giftshop. Some of the things you can purchase include the rental of a Rolls Royce Silver Shadow or 2000 Bentley Azure convertible, a $400 marabou feather vest, or a pair of 24-carat gold handcuffs. There are even penthouses for sale, in case you decide that you quite like Miami and Mondrian style and feel like purchasing some of the drama for yourself.

Photography courtesy Morgans Hotel Group

MIAMI BEACH_FLORIDA, LOS ANGELES_CALIFORNIA, PALM SPRINGS_CALI
SARANAC LAKE_NEW YORK, MIAMI BEACH_FLORIDA GREENOUGH_MONTANA, MIAMI
NANTUCKET_MASSACHUSETTS PALM SPRINGS_CALIFORNIA, LOS ANGELES_CALIFORNI
SEATTLE_WASHINGTON KEY WEST_FLORIDA, JACKSON_WYOMING ISLAMORADA_FLOR
PORTLAND_OREGON, MIAMI BEACH_FLORIDA, LITTLE TORCH KEY_FLORIDA, MIAMI
BEACH_FLORIDA, LOS ANGELES_CALIFORNIA, PALM SPRINGS_CALIFORNIA, HARBOU
YORK, MIAMI BEACH_FLORIDA GREENOUGH_MONTANA, MIAMI BEACH_FLORIDA, NA
SPRINGS_CALIFORNIA, LOS ANGELES_CALIFORNIA MIAMI BEACH_FLORIDA, MORRIS
JACKSON_WYOMING ISLAMORADA_FLORIDA, NEW YORK_NEW YORK, MIAMI BEACH_F
KEY_FLORIDA, MIAMI BEACH_FLORIDA, PALM SPRINGS_CALIFORNIA NEW YORK_NEW
SPRINGS_CALIFORNIA, HARBOUR ISLAND_THE BAHAMAS NEW YORK_NEW YORK, LON
MIAMI BEACH_FLORIDA, NANTUCKET_MASSACHUSETTS MIAMI BEACH_FLORIDA PALM
BEACH_FLORIDA, MORRIS_CONNECTICUT BOSTON_MASSACHUSETTS, PORTLAND_ORE
MIAMI BEACH_FLORIDA DOLORES_COLORADO SANTA BARBARA_CALIFORNIA, PORTLA
NEW YORK_NEW YORK, HARBOUR ISLAND_THE BAHAMAS, MIAMI BEACH_FLORIDA, L
ISLAND_NEW YORK ISLAMORADA_FLORIDA, SARANAC LAKE_NEW YORK, MIAMI BEAC
SPRINGS_CALIFORNIA, NANTUCKET_MASSACHUSETTS PALM SPRINGS_CALIFORNIA, LO
SEATTLE_WASHINGTON KEY WEST_FLORIDA, JACKSON_WYOMING ISLAMORADA_FLOR
PORTLAND_OREGON, MIAMI BEACH_FLORIDA, LITTLE TORCH KEY_FLORIDA, MIAMI
BEACH_FLORIDA, LOS ANGELES_CALIFORNIA, PALM SPRINGS_CALIFORNIA, HARBOU
YORK, MIAMI BEACH_FLORIDA GREENOUGH_MONTANA, MIAMI BEACH_FLORIDA, NA
SPRINGS_CALIFORNIA, LOS ANGELES_CALIFORNIA MIAMI BEACH_FLORIDA, MORRIS
JACKSON_WYOMING ISLAMORADA_FLORIDA, NEW YORK_NEW YORK, MIAMI BEACH_F
KEY_FLORIDA, MIAMI BEACH_FLORIDA, PALM SPRINGS_CALIFORNIA NEW YORK_NEW
SPRINGS_CALIFORNIA, HARBOUR ISLAND_THE BAHAMAS NEW YORK_NEW YORK, LON
MIAMI BEACH_FLORIDA, NANTUCKET_MASSACHUSETTS MIAMI BEACH_FLORIDA PALM
BEACH_FLORIDA, MORRIS_CONNECTICUT BOSTON_MASSACHUSETTS, PORTLAND_ORE
MIAMI BEACH_FLORIDA DOLORES_COLORADO SANTA BARBARA_CALIFORNIA, PORTLA
NEW YORK_NEW YORK, HARBOUR ISLAND_THE BAHAMAS, MIAMI BEACH_FLORIDA, L
ISLAND_NEW YORK ISLAMORADA_FLORIDA, SARANAC LAKE_NEW YORK, MIAMI BEAC
SPRINGS_CALIFORNIA, NANTUCKET_MASSACHUSETTS PALM SPRINGS_CALIFORNIA, LO
SEATTLE_WASHINGTON KEY WEST_FLORIDA, JACKSON_WYOMING ISLAMORADA_FLOR
PORTLAND_OREGON, MIAMI BEACH_FLORIDA, LITTLE TORCH KEY_FLORIDA, MIAMI
BEACH_FLORIDA, LOS ANGELES_CALIFORNIA, PALM SPRINGS_CALIFORNIA, HARBOU
YORK, MIAMI BEACH_FLORIDA GREENOUGH_MONTANA, MIAMI BEACH_FLORIDA, NA
SPRINGS_CALIFORNIA, LOS ANGELES_CALIFORNIA MIAMI BEACH_FLORIDA, MORRIS
JACKSON_WYOMING ISLAMORADA_FLORIDA, NEW YORK_NEW YORK, MIAMI BEACH
KEY_FLORIDA, MIAMI BEACH_FLORIDA, PALM SPRINGS_CALIFORNIA NEW YORK_NEW
SPRINGS_CALIFORNIA, HARBOUR ISLAND_THE BAHAMAS NEW YORK_NEW YORK, LON
MIAMI BEACH_FLORIDA, NANTUCKET_MASSACHUSETTS MIAMI BEACH_FLORIDA PALM
BEACH_FLORIDA, MORRIS_CONNECTICUT BOSTON_MASSACHUSETTS, PORTLAND_ORE
MIAMI BEACH_FLORIDA DOLORES_COLORADO SANTA BARBARA_CALIFORNIA, PORTLA
NEW YORK_NEW YORK, HARBOUR ISLAND_THE BAHAMAS, MIAMI BEACH_FLORIDA, L
ISLAND_NEW YORK ISLAMORADA_FLORIDA, SARANAC LAKE_NEW YORK, MIAMI BEAC
SPRINGS_CALIFORNIA, NANTUCKET_MASSACHUSETTS PALM SPRINGS_CALIFORNIA, L
SEATTLE_WASHINGTON KEY WEST_FLORIDA, JACKSON_WYOMING ISLAMORADA_FLOR
PORTLAND_OREGON, MIAMI BEACH_FLORIDA, LITTLE TORCH KEY_FLORIDA, MIAMI
BEACH_FLORIDA, LOS ANGELES_CALIFORNIA, PALM SPRINGS_CALIFORNIA, HARBOU
YORK, MIAMI BEACH_FLORIDA GREENOUGH_MONTANA, MIAMI BEACH_FLORIDA, NA
SPRINGS_CALIFORNIA, LOS ANGELES_CALIFORNIA MIAMI BEACH_FLORIDA, MORRIS
JACKSON_WYOMING ISLAMORADA_FLORIDA, NEW YORK_NEW YORK, MIAMI BEACH,
KEY_FLORIDA, MIAMI BEACH_FLORIDA, PALM SPRINGS_CALIFORNIA NEW YORK_NEW
SPRINGS_CALIFORNIA, HARBOUR ISLAND_THE BAHAMAS NEW YORK_NEW YORK, LON

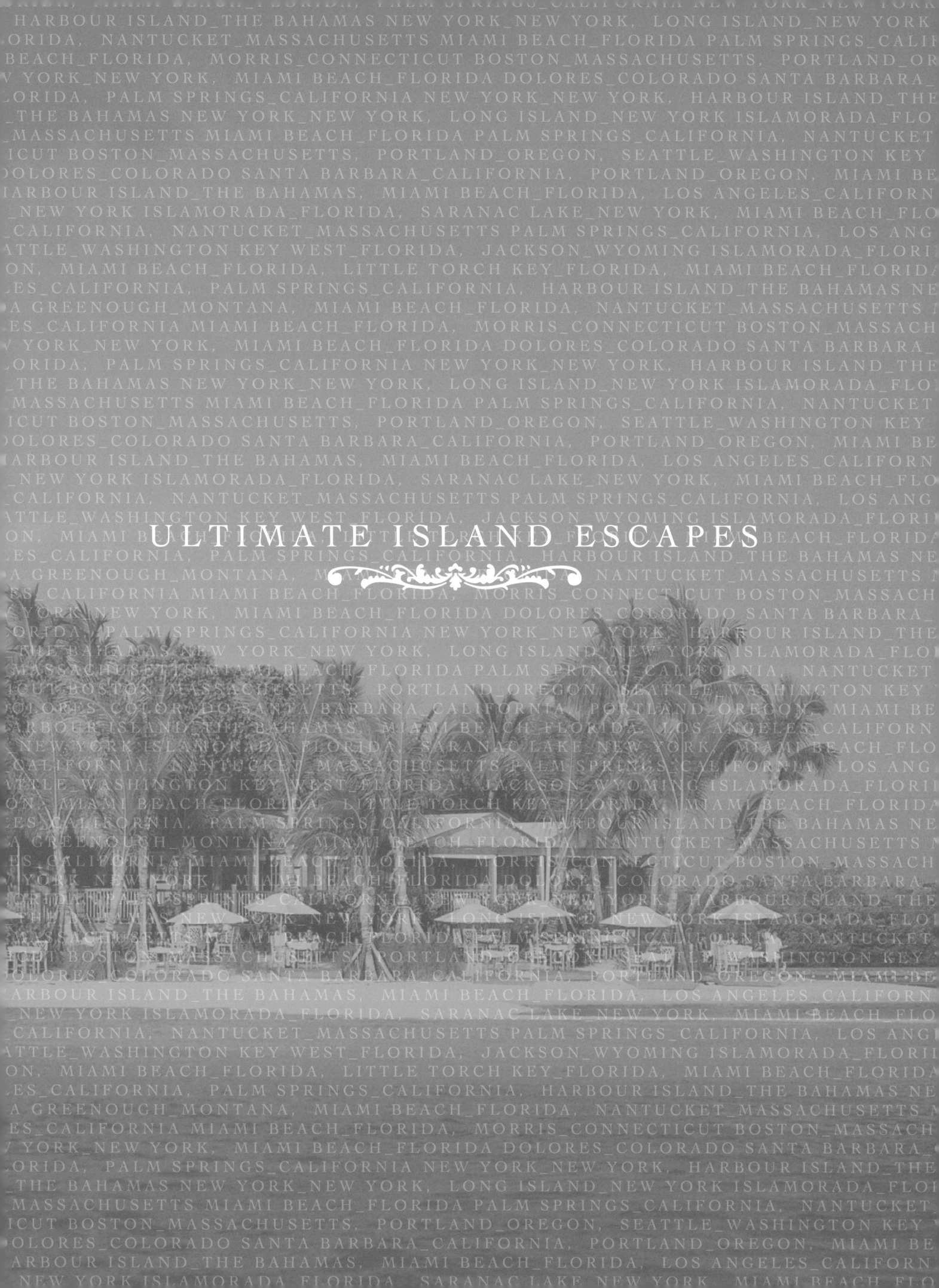

ULTIMATE ISLAND ESCAPES

- Architecture/Design: Southern meets West Indies Colonial
- Highlight: The hammock on the end of the pier
- To pack: A cool straw hat

THE MOORINGS

Islamorada, Florida Keys, Florida

Set at the very end of the USA in a place that time forgot, the Florida Keys is an achingly beautiful string of islands joined by the famous island-to-island Overseas Highway that is quite possibly one of the most picturesque in the world. Although renowned for its scenery—spectacular vistas of ocean greet you as you cruise down the Keys—the region is also noted for being peppered with sublime island architecture. Indeed, some people travel here to see the gingerbread-style beach houses as much as the sea, taking time to wander up and down the Keys in search of these simple wooden residences bursting with charm, color, and character.

Ranging from gracious, well-proportioned sea captains' houses to more modest cottages with porches and winking cheeriness, these distinctive homes have a Bahamian flavor flowing through their architectural vernacular with turquoise, pink, and sea-blue shades creating an ice-cream-bright palette and decorative balustrades and fretwork providing ornamental elegance. Together, these elements have helped define the style that has become known as the Key West.

Halfway down the Keys, between Key Largo and Key West, is a group of islands called Islamorada, a quiet settlement with a sprinkling of these beach retreats. It was on one of these, Upper Matecombe, that Frenchman Hubert Baudoin washed ashore after traveling around the world. He immediately fell in love with this environment, its Caribbean influences, and its eccentric outpost-style character, and decided to build his dream escape. The property he bought was located in a prime position on the beach and had existed as a private estate since 1936. At the time, it came with planning permission for 250 holiday units—each with an ocean view—but Baudoin didn't want to spoil the untouched nature of this idyllic hideaway, so he decided to draw up plans for a more sympathetic retreat instead; one that left the coconut groves and the sugar-white beach in pristine condition. The result was The Moorings, one of the most enchanting places in the Keys, if not the entire American East Coast.

Set back from the 1,100-foot private beach—one of the best in the Keys—among a landscape of swaying palms and meandering pathways leading through the grass to the sand are a collection of postcard-perfect cottages, all constructed in a slightly different architectural design but all with a chic, plantation house-style feel. Each cottage faces the beach, but they are also set within their own space to ensure privacy and a measure of aesthetics. Guests often comment that it's like staying at their own secluded beach hideaway, only with hotel facilities at hand.

Four original cottages date back to the 1930s; the other houses were built in the early 1990s, but even the modern ones have a reassuringly traditional feel. Some are whitewashed, while others are enhanced with fuschia-pink, turquoise, or Tiffany-blue touches. Most feature shutters that blink sleepily in the sun and enticing wraparound verandas that encourage siestas on wicker chairs. Inside, each is just as stylish, with colonial-style furnishings and rooms that often include four-poster beds designed for deep slumber.

The Moorings is so pretty, it's no wonder designers and photographers are often here using the estate for photo shoots. There is a 1950s-style glamour to the scene: an old wooden boat waits patiently on the sand for its sailor and white yachts are moored in front of the beach, while a beautifully weathered pier with a hammock, a view of the Atlantic Ocean, and a pervading atmosphere of serenity put the final exclamation mark on a scene that is as close to island perfection as you can imagine. This is beach architecture at its most inspirational.

The Moorings has delivered what many of us have been longing for: a place to escape modern life and return to a simpler, old-fashioned style of existence, where the only worries we might face are those pertaining to which wine we might drink and what time to meander down to the hammock, with a glass and a book in hand.

Photography courtesy Janelle McCulloch

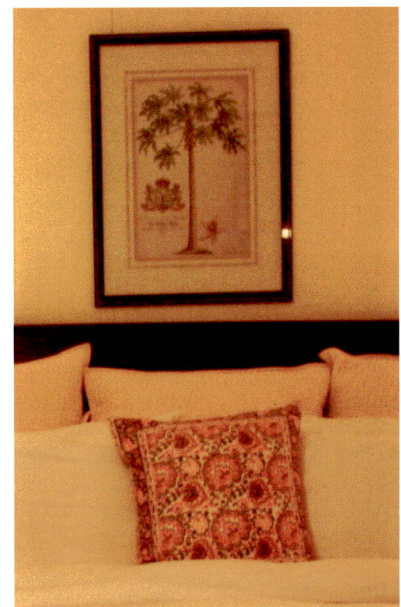

- Architecture/Design: Classic Americana meets beach house chic
- Highlight: The proximity to Nantucket's shops and harbor
- To pack: Binoculars, for the veiws
- Note: November to mid May

THE VERANDA HOUSE

Nantucket, Massachusetts

There is something quintessentially American about The Veranda House. Perhaps it's the crisp swathes of red and white throughout, heralding a kind of patriotic welcome, or maybe it's the beautifully simple Colonial-style furniture and paintings set in strategic, almost Shakerish, positions for full effect. Or it may simply be the island of Nantucket itself, one of America's most charming destinations. Whatever it is, The Veranda House is so elegant it's as if Ralph Lauren himself had played a part in creating this ultimate American summer getaway.

Perched high on one of Nantucket's enchanting cobblestone streets, where its landmark, naturally weathered porches overlook the cool blue views of the famous harbor and sea, the 18-room guesthouse began life in the early 1800s as The Overlook, a getaway catering to wealthy mainlanders who journeyed to the island for some invigorating sea air. Although it stoically withstood both sea air and demanding guests for the next two centuries and underwent restoration in the 1950s, by 2002 the guesthouse was no longer suited to modern times and a new generation of discerning guests accustomed to a highly designed hotel style.

When the new owners took over in the early 2000s, they thoroughly assessed this grand, rambling, labyrinthine mansion and saw that the gingerbread-trim verandas were still intact and that its architectural structure was still solid. This, in turn, made them realize that the property's potential lay not in the undertaking of a total renovation, but in the restoration of the building to its former grandeur, while adding a modern kick. In short, it needed an injection of hip.

They also realized that the definitive word was hip because with so many other hotels on the island aiming for the chintz-chic look, there was a real need for a destination that was a little different. But how to tread that fine line between achieving a cutting-edge contemporary look and keeping the integrity and personality of the endearing property? The answer was in a subtle refit. Out went any stuffy furnishings and the outdated carpet, which was pulled up to reveal beautiful hardwood, wide-plank pine flooring, most likely brought to the island on whaling ships, and in came the builders.

Both floors and walls were stripped back and repainted or polished to leave a clean canvas for a revised beach aesthetic. Rooms were updated so that each featured a modern ensuite with Italian rain showers, and then luxuries such as Frette linens, Simon Pearce lamps, exquisite down comforters, antique photos in sophisticated frames, bathrobes, and cute baskets with red beach towels were added to the mix. The owners were careful to keep the entire look clean, elegant, and simple. The three wraparound verandas with their gingerbread trim were kept just as they were, as each offered a perfect vantage to sit and sip G&Ts at dusk while adding a distinguished air to the property, and the shingle façade was also retained. The final result was a place that was both simple and sophisticated. Just as a good beach retreat should be.

There are still fragments of the old guesthouse remaining—the floorboards creak good-naturedly and you have to walk up stairs to reach your room rather than catch an elevator—but guests love these aspects just as much as the new touches. The best thing about The Veranda House, though, is the service, which is not only impeccable but also imbued with personal touches. Afternoon tea with freshly baked cookies is served every day on the main veranda in front of the foyer; breakfast, taken downstairs in a black-and-white dining room, is a similarly luxurious affair; and while evening meals are taken off-site in one of the island's many restaurants or pubs, the concierge and staff are happy to offer suggestions on the most suitable establishments.

There are many places to stay on Nantucket, one of America's most popular summer destinations, next to Martha's Vineyard, the Hamptons, Miami, and Maine, but there is something rather special about The Veranda House. It has both a picture-perfect charm and a winking cheeriness that draws you in and makes you wish you could stay in this magical place forever.

Photography courtesy Rare Brick

■ Architecture/Design: Clifftop drama
■ Highlight: The view from the restaurant
■ To pack: Your conversation skills—cocktail hour is always great here

ROCK HOUSE

Harbour Island, the Bahamas

When Rock House opened on Harbour Island in 2002, it immediately caused a stir in both the Bahamas and across the sea in Miami. Its owner was Miami developer J. Wallace Tutt, who had already achieved a level of fame for his previous projects, which included Casa Casuarina, the Miami mansion owned by the late Gianni Versace and a house for Cher. Tutt, who doesn't like to do things quietly, saw the potential of Rock House, which had previously existed as a private residence and then a B&B. Together with his partner, Don Purdy, he decided to inject some Miami-style glamour into the property. The result is an island hideaway that is like few others in the Bahamas.

Perched on the edge of a cliff, overlooking an impressive view of the bay, the hotel is spectacular—and raises eyebrows from the moment you walk through the front gate. The principal public rooms, including the dining room, the reading room, and the soigné restaurant terrace, are designed on a grand scale. Each features antique furniture and accessories that look like they belong in a country estate, and yet each feels surprisingly welcoming and comfortable.

No expense has been spared with the redesign, and it is in the rooms and suites that this becomes utterly apparent. Each has been decorated in an upscale casual style, which essentially means layers of luxury done in a very understated way. Think tasteful teak, bamboo and rattan furnishings, elegant fabrics, art books, and vintage island photographs and maps. Some of the rooms face the ocean, others have a garden outlook—all of them have the feel of a private home.

Outside, the expansive courtyard that surrounds the pool is dotted with stylish, private cabanas, where guests can find some peace with a good book and a cool drink any time of the day. Some of the rooms also have their own private cabanas, which have been decked out with soft daybeds and fancy lamps. The predominant colors of Rock House are red and canary yellow, and the combination is both bright and playful.

Since it opened, Rock House has been frequented by many celebrity guests, from Lenny Kravitz to Elle Macpherson and Robert DeNiro, and you can see why. Rock House is a boutique hotel with the all the qualities of a five-star establishment, but it feels more like a very plush private home. If only we could move in for good.

Photography courtesy Janelle McCulloch and Cookie Kinkead

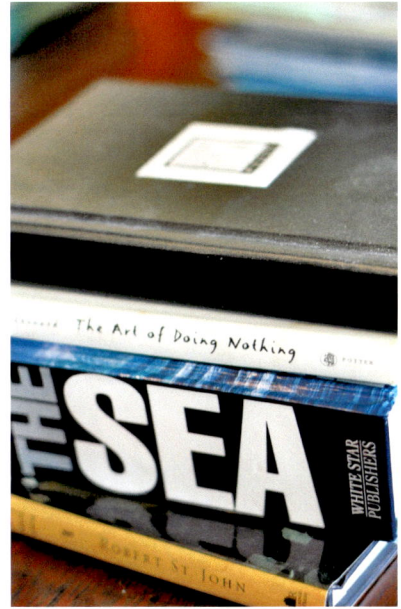

LITTLE PALM ISLAND

Little Torch Key, Florida

Little Palm Island is like *Gilligan's Island* with a *Forbes 500* cast, marooned on an island with a yacht full of top-notch supplies. Almost as famous for its distinguished guests, former Presidents Harry Truman, Theodore Roosevelt, and John F. Kennedy among them, as for its location—a glittering 5.5-acre idyll off the Florida Keys—Little Palm Island is one of America's most sublime island escapes.

To reach Little Palm Island, you first need to make your way down the Keys, island-by-island, and then leave your car at Little Torch Key and take a seaplane or be shuttled across in the beautiful, 35-foot, wood-lined launch *The Truman*, reveling in the seclusion and scenery. If you see a fin rise suddenly up out of the water, don't worry: it's not uncommon for dolphins to escort the boat over to the island. There are no televisions or alarm clocks here—such unnecessary accessories are discouraged—so the only sound you'll hear as you step out of the boat is birdsong underscored with the gentle lapping of waves.

The architectural style is British Colonial meets island fantasy, with an emphasis firmly on the fantasy. Each of the 28 bungalows has a thatched roof on top and island-style beds inside—four-poster, with canopies and netting—with mahogany furnishings and candles to light the rooms at night, plus a veranda and hammock in which to lie and soak up the sea view. There are spa baths in the bathrooms, but many guests love using the outdoor showers behind the bamboo fences. The lush foliage and groves of Jamaican coconut palms offer privacy while the flowering tropical plants add scented ambience. It's like the perfect Caribbean hideaway, only you don't have to leave the US to get there.

There is also a spa, a pool, and other activities such as sailing and diving to indulge in, but most guests here are content to simply lie in one of the oversized hammocks strung between the trees or embrace the crystal blue waters. Little Palm Island reminds guests of the beauty of simplicity, of how life was before deadlines and stress got in the way.

Okay, so not everything's simple: breakfast may be an asparagus and caviar omelet with some chilled Veuve Cliquot Champagne. Dinner is even more elaborate and guests often elect to take it at their own table on the beach. But at night when the island descends into darkness, the candles are lit, the moon highlights the sea, and the gentle Key Deer swim over from neighboring islands, Little Palm Island really does become the most perfect, untouched paradise, far removed from it all.

Photography courtesy Little Palm Island Resort & Spa

MILL HOUSE INN

East Hampton, Long Island, New York

The Hamptons needs no introduction, they have been part of the myth of Manhattan for as long as people have been seeking to escape New York for the weekend. They're a place to retreat to at the end of Long Island for some peace, beach bliss, and architectural eye candy, before throwing yourself back into the frenzied pace of the city again. The Hamptons appeal to New Yorkers because they're a charming mixture of juxtapositions: rural scenery and farmgates selling fresh produce on one side and hedonism in homes the other. And while manicured privet hedges conceal some of the region, most of it is blissfully open for prime viewing. Take a wander through East Hampton or along one of the magnificent stretches of beach and you're likely to see someone wealthy and/or famous at play, any time of the day or year.

The true appeal of the Hamptons, though, is the authenticity and spirit. It's easy to forget there's authenticity here, underneath the oceanfront mansions and new Mercedes Benz, but the Hamptons are very real. The tree-trimmed streets, the cute ponds, the quaint villages, the spectacular coastline, and the rambling country roads create a unique community that is held in place by a sense of history and residents determined to keep it the same, no matter how much wealth flows in.

Some of this authenticity can be found at what is one of the Hamptons' prettiest hideaways, the Mill House Inn, an historic property dating from 1790. Set in East Hampton, arguably the Hamptons' prettiest village, on the South Fork of Long Island, it was named as "One of the Fifty Top Small Hotels in the US" by Zagat's 2008 survey. It is a curious and intriguing place: an historic windmill, the Old Hook Windmill, stands tall and proud beside it, protecting a small cemetery to the other side, but neither of these two quirky features seem alarming beside the Mill House Inn, which adeptly brings the whole scene together with architectural integrity and charm.

Originally built by the Parsons Family in 1790, the house passed into several more families before becoming a guesthouse in 1973. It was only when current owners Sylvia and Gary Muller purchased it in 1999 that the two-century-old estate was restored, upgraded, and then restored again, becoming what it is today: a deliciously different Hamptons hideaway that perfectly captures the essence of this region.

Occupying a 19th-century house are 10 individually decorated rooms that somehow achieve that fine balance between traditional and modern. The two suites in the recent addition behind the main house have fireplaces and bathrooms big enough to ride a bike in, but it is the interior design of this destination that is really appealing. Some of the rooms, such as the America's Cup Suite, are decorated in a cheerily nautical red, white, and blue theme that doesn't seem twee, but classic American. The Captain's Suite, meanwhile, has a collection of antiques that looks like a captain has gathered during his round-the-world voyages, while the Hemingway Suite is a tribute to the great writer, complete with colonial-style furnishings and African pieces. The Beach Hampton Suite is designed in the manner of an elegant beach house with all-white rooms and white

timber furniture, and the Hampton Classic was inspired by the equestrian event and has been decorated in rich thoroughbred colors. Other accommodations have beautiful old leather sofas, framed antique maps, and grand old iron beds. Overall, it is a design that never wanders over into mediocrity or "old B&B" territory, but stays firmly on the side of sophistication.

Even the verandah, dressed in Adirondack chairs for reading or sipping G&Ts, is something you'd love to have on your own house—together with the inn's dog, Cory, who gleefully welcomes everyone in sight. Set so close to the beach you could wander down before breakfast, the Mill House Inn is a place for respite and restoration. The light, the quiet, the peace, and the design all conspire to make you relax, and get into the Hamptons spirit.

Photography courtesy Sylvia Muller

THE LANDING

Harbour Island, the Bahamas

In the late 1990s, Australian businessman Toby Tyler and his wife, the Bahamian-born New York-based model Tracy Barry, who had met on a blind date in Sydney, decided to restore an old family estate on Harbour Island in the Bahamas. Their original plan had been to sell the estate, which Barry had owned for some years, but when they traveled to the island to assess the property and found themselves standing in front of two of the most architecturally significant buildings in the Bahamas, on an island that is often voted the prettiest in the greater Caribbean, they decided to put down their bags and stay instead. As Tyler says: "I fell in love twice; once with my wife, and then with her island."

Harbour Island is everything you imagine a tiny Bahamian island to be. Dubbed "the Nantucket of the Caribbean" for its shady lanes and pastel-painted, New England-style clapboard cottages, it is famous worldwide for its beaches and its celebrity guests. But it is also gaining a well-deserved reputation for its architecture, which is one part classic, plantation-style elegance, one part Cape Cod-style simplicity, and one part Caribbean charm. Standing tall over the harbor as the first sight for visitors as they arrive by water taxi to the island (the only way of reaching this idyllic outpost), The Landing hotel epitomizes Harbour Island's unique architectural style. Built in 1800, the hotel has a distinct poise and dignity, but it also has a sense of humor—a winking Caribbean-style cheekiness—that shines through the elegant façade.

The hotel's beauty is testament to the talents of its owners and also to the talents of their designer, India Hicks, daughter of famed London designer David Hicks, who also lives on Harbour Island and who helped bring The Landing back to life. Together with Hicks, Tyler and Barry took on the restoration and redesign of The Landing's two buildings: an 1820 plantation-style house and a neighboring 1820 property called The Captain's House. Having survived more than a century of harsh weather, the white limestone and clapboard-sided buildings were solid but desperately in need of care.

Determined to retain the elegant and understated feel of the architecture and its airy breezeways, high ceilings, polished hardwood floors, and wraparound verandas, the three set about restoring the buildings using local craftsmen and the finest materials to create two classic, plantation-style island retreats.

Hicks sourced chic colonial furnishings to create bedrooms that look as though they were lifted from a fashion shoot, while Tyler set out turning the restaurant into one of the most talked about in this part of the world.

In keeping with the idea of a colonial idyll, they enhanced the wide wooden verandas that surround both buildings at the front and then decorated the interior in white-on-white, with rich, dark chocolate timber for contrast. In each of the bedrooms, crisp white shutters provide relief from the sun, while ceiling fans, seagrass mats, and four-poster beds with cool linens combine to provide a welcome haven for guests morning, noon, or night. Now one of the most famous hotels and restaurants in the Bahamas, The Landing hotel and restaurant are a tribute to the endurance of love, architecture, and the alluring dream of living, if only for a short time, in an island paradise.

Photography courtesy Janelle McCulloch

- Architecture/Design: Pared-back glamour
- Highlight: The island bar and pool—set on its own little key
- To pack: A camera—the sunsets are magical

CASA MORADA

Islamorada, Florida Keys

Casa Morada, located in Islamorada, halfway down the Florida Keys, is the work of three talented and ambitious women—former New Yorkers Lauren Abrams, Terry Ford, and Heide Werthamer. The trio, who had previously worked for hotel legend Ian Schrager at the Delano, Morgans, Royalton, and Mondrian hotels, spent a considerable amount of time searching the Keys for a hotel to call their own. When they bought this property in 2002, a 1.7-acre estate on the Gulf Shore side of Islamorada, they knew they had found a diamond in the rough.

Everything about this fabulous place has been carefully thought out, from the style to the architecture to the atmosphere, and because of this it tends to appeal to design lovers and the magazine crowd. But they're not the only guests enamored of Casa Morada—people are traveling from all corners of the globe for this finely tuned, luxurious experience. Right from the moment you check in—at an indoor–outdoor reception area cooled by sea breezes and decked out with a swinging chair, a white fiberglass Eames chaise, and complimentary bicycles—you know this hotel is going to be a little different. The beauty of the place is that it's architectural and hip and slick—all those things that modern design lovers like—but it's also low key and laid back. It's a hideaway in every sense of the word and naturally and architecturally beautiful from every angle.

The previous owner had tried to convert the former 1950s motel, originally named the Sunset Inn, into a more upmarket retreat and had already spent a lot of time and money on the place, but Abrams, Ford, and Werthamer knew what needed to be done to really elevate it to another level of glamour. They took the nondescript, white, two-story buildings and pared them back so that the lines were cleaner and then gave them a lick of whiter-than-white paint so that it all appeared even more brilliant and modern. They then turned their attention to the rooms. As part of injecting a vibrant, new personality into the place, the rooms were given names instead of numbers—such as Starfish and Iguana—and each was renovated with smart new bamboo floors, luxurious baths, and mahogany beds. The rest of the hotel's spaces were then dressed in a romantic mix of colonial and modern furniture and a library of carefully selected books to read. As a final touch, they added private terraces, verandas, or gardens to each suite, because after all, one of the real pleasures of being in the Keys is spending time outside.

The best bit of Casa Morada, however, comes last. Set at the rear of the property, on its own little key in Florida Bay, the pool and bar area is Casa's showpiece. "We really loved this part of the property when we saw it," says Abrams. "This area was what really was sold it to us. We knew we could do amazing things with it." And they have. The group brought in renowned Miami landscape architect Raymond Jungles to revamp the pleasure island, and his suggestion was to keep it as lovely and low key as the rest of the place. Now reached by a cute white timber footbridge and encircled by palm trees, the area features an all-white timber bar set out over the water, a scattering of white deckchairs and chaise longues, a timber tower (full of cushions for people who want to escape the heat), a cute pool, and a shimmering view of the sea.

Casa Morada has become a preferred backdrop for many magazine photographers and it's easy to see why—the entire hotel is a stylist's dream. One reviewer described Casa Morada as "a secluded jewel of a resort where magic happens", and that is entirely believable. At the end of the day, when the sun glows red and then sinks peacefully over the ocean, offering a perfect scene from the bar or the poolside loungers, there's surely no better place to be on the Keys.

Photography courtesy Janelle McCulloch

ALEXANDER'S GUESTHOUSE

Key West, Florida

The famous Overseas Highway from Miami to Key West is one of the world's great drives. It's a magical, island-to-island journey that takes you over 42 bridges, each more beautiful than the last and each allowing a glimpse of the shimmering sea as you wind your way from key to key, until you finally reach the end of the road—Key West. The southernmost point of the USA, Key West is a brightly painted, slightly eccentric, character-filled place that shimmers with flamboyant style and tropical pleasures—the kind of place where you pluck out a loud shirt, order up a frozen margarita or a Key lime pie, and kick back to embrace the fun and sun. Not surprisingly, most things here are loud or colorful or both, and very few things in Key West are understated. Except, of course, Alexander's Guesthouse.

An architectural anomaly, Alexander's Guesthouse is a slice of white sophistication in a town known for its rainbow shades. Owned by one of the most stylish couples in Miami, it has a quiet, monochromatic glamour and simple but beautiful interior design that has helped it establish a reputation for being one of Florida's, if not North America's, most elegant hideaways. If you want gaudy, you'll need to head further down the Main Street; and if it's antiques you want, you'd better find a different B&B. The only thing loud or bright at Alexander's is the tomato juice in their killer Bloody Mary.

Built in the early 1900s in the historic Old Town district, the hotel consists of two guesthouses located side by side. Owned by two sisters (each had a house), the properties were eventually sold to different owners. Years on, after the properties had changed hands several times, an architect came along, saw the potential in rejoining the properties and decided to reunite the two houses. Fortunately, the renovation not only retained the gracious character and fine lines of the two buildings but also injected a bit of modern hip. The hotel is now spread over three buildings—the two original houses and another at the back of the property—and anchored by a pool, a hot tub, and a fabulously convivial poolside bar in the center. Mingling is mandatory at the poolside happy hour every afternoon and the frozen piña coladas are another must-do.

Apart from the luscious green garden, which is filled with palms, bougainvillea, hibiscus, and banana, and the fruity drinks, the predominant colors of Alexander's are black and white, a palette that adds a heightened level of sophistication to the hotel. Each of the rooms is decorated with black armchairs and white linens, an effect that comes off as modern but not stark, and the public areas are equally stylish—so much so that they look like spreads from a lifestyle magazine. Some of the rooms have French doors opening to the courtyard/pool area and some have their own balconies for private sunbathing

Alexander's is a rare gem. A serene retreat in every sense of the word, it allows guests to go out and have their Key West fun, knowing there's a quiet place to rest their heads at the end of the day. Many guests book in for two days and end up staying a week. After tasting the piña coladas, it's easy to see why.

Photography courtesy Janelle McCulloch

UNION STREET INN

Nantucket, Massachusetts

There's just one word for the Union Street Inn—impeccable. Presided over by two equally impeccable innkeepers, Ken and Deb Withrow, who cut their teeth on top New York hotels and high-end retail display, it's a perfect mix of 18th-century architecture and 21st-century service, of classic style and modern luxuries, of old-fashioned charm and present-day conveniences. Most of the guests who stay here return year after year and, not surprisingly, many guests wish they could just unpack their bags and reside here permanently. It's that kind of place.

Built in 1770, the inn is an integral part of Nantucket's history. Located a few cobblestones from the centre of town, the building stands as strong as it did more than two centuries ago, thanks to solid foundations and a lot of love and care by the owners over the years. A must for lovers of historic architecture, it still has the old servants' passages and stairs that sneak between the rooms and floors, the wide plank floors, the gracious rooms, and of course the colonial grandeur that distinguishes many of the buildings in this graceful town. Since taking over the 14-room inn a decade or so ago, the Withrows have restored and redecorated on several occasions—most recently in 2000—but to their credit they haven't wallpapered over the history or the personality of the place. In fact, the new interior design has only added to the beauty, intimacy, style, and charm.

Many of the rooms have functioning wood-burning fireplaces and are outfitted with Oriental rugs, handsome wing armchairs, and grand four-poster or canopied beds, each dressed with Frette linens and plump eiderdowns. The public areas are as welcoming as a private home, complete with Boston and New York newspapers waiting to be read in the sitting areas, an elegant desk with courtesy laptop and phone for guests' use, and a basket of umbrellas by the front door. Even at the breakfast table it feels as though you're in someone's home. Included in the price, breakfast is superb, with either hot or cold dishes of French toast, eggs, fruit, or apple cinnamon pancakes. The kitchen is open to guests all day long; at night, when most of them return from dining out in town, many help themselves to a cup of tea and home-made chocolate chip cookies before retiring to their fireplace-warmed rooms.

The Union Street Inn describes itself as a "classic Nantucket bed and breakfast," but it's so much more than that. It's an inn with heart and soul and grace—a place where you go to feel loved and cosseted. There are so many new, modern, edgy, and occasionally soulless hotels being built on both coasts of the USA that when you come across one with a true sense of history and charm, it feels like a true breath of fresh air. If only more "inns" could be like this.

Photography courtesy Janelle McCulloch

ARCHITECTURAL MUST-SEES

- Architecture/Design: Desert mirage-fabulous
- Highlight: The poolside delights
- To pack: Your swing—Palm Springs is famous for its golf courses

VICEROY PALM SPRINGS

Palm Springs, California

How absolutely exquisite is the Viceroy Palm Springs? It comes across as being the model of discretion, a well-groomed, beautifully turned out, charmingly polite place, but then it winks at you in such a way as to suggest that it may also have the most delicious, wicked sense of humor underneath. "Come in," it says, "I'll pour you a wine ... unless you want to go straight to a stiff martini?"

Look up the Viceroy's saucy provenance, however, and you can see why it might be inclined to misbehave. The hotel started life as a place where Hollywood came to play, out here in the desert. It saw it all—and then some more besides. Then, when it was taken over by the KOR Hotels Group and given a makeover by Kelly Wearstler, people took a cautious step backwards. Would it be the same, they wondered? Would it have that same welcoming atmosphere? Well, the new hotel is very different from the old one—the design is high-glamour-meets-Wearstler-whimsy—but there are still glimpses of the cheeky, party-lovin' old gal that people remember.

The color scheme is based on a cheesy, breakfast-bright, yolk-yellow-and-white palette that's immediately uplifting, and although the décor feels very surreal, it is also quite fabulous. The sun shines almost all the time in Palm Springs, but it literally emanates from the furniture at the Viceroy. There are touches of black-and-white gingham to tone down the cheeriness but by and large the yellow dominates as much as the sun. And you know what? It feels fitting. Very Palm Springs.

The key to the Viceroy is its retro edge, an edge that sits perfectly in this town, which seems straight out of a time warp. Palm Springs is soaked in history and many of the town's ghosts seem to linger, even the streets are named after the stars who came here to party—Sinatra, President Ford, Charlie Chaplin, Ginger Rogers, Humphrey Bogart, Lucille Ball. They all came, played, stayed, played some more, and in the process created a destination of mythical status. In Palm Springs, you feel like doing things you've never imagined doing before, whether it's dancing all night, going for a midnight skinny dip in a kidney shaped pool, playing golf wearing plaid, or just drinking your weight in cocktails. And the Viceroy is a resort that encourages you every step of the way. In fact, the hotel starts off the party by providing

lobster barbecues by the pool, free bicycles on which to get around town, and a day spa to recover from it all afterward. They'll even give you an aromatherapy massage under the stars—and Palm Springs' night sky is truly amazing.

Some of those who have lingered at the hotel in its former life include Errol Flynn and several American presidents—they knew a good thing when they saw it. It doesn't get much more fabulous than Palm Springs, and it doesn't get much more stylish than the Viceroy. Put some Sinatra on your iPod, mix some cocktails, and soak up the scene with glee.

Photography courtesy KOR Hotel Group

- Architecture/Design: Pure Sinatra
- Highlight: The piano-shaped pool
- To pack: Sinatra CDs, of course

TWIN PALMS

Palm Springs, California

Frank Sinatra knew how to throw a party. And he wasn't too bad at singing a tune either. But he also knew how to design a house. In 1947, flush with his first million, he strode into the architectural firm of Williams, Williams & Williams licking an ice cream and commissioned a project—a mid-century modern home for his family. He had ideas, of course—Sinatra always had grand ideas—but few could have imagined that the King of Croon could have envisaged such an extraordinary space.

The design, by the now-famous architect E. Stewart Williams, cost Sinatra $150,000. Because the singer wanted it by Christmas, the firm employed builders around the clock, although this still wasn't enough and it took until New Year's Eve to complete. Which, in the end, suited Sinatra just fine. He was ready to celebrate.

Twin Palms immediately became the Mecca for Frank's Rat Pack pals and the rest of Hollywood's elite. Although small by celebrity standards, the 4,500-square-foot home was the perfect party pad, with a piano-shaped pool, complete with a specially designed walkway that created the piano keys when the sun shone through the holes, a flagpole to raise the banner when Happy Hour was about to begin each afternoon, and an interior fit for Sinatra.

But it wasn't to be a happy home for the blue-eyed legend. When he fell in love with Ava Gardner and she moved in after Sinatra had left his wife, Twin Palms became the scene for some of their most violent fights—one of the bathroom basins still carries a crack from a champagne bottle that he hurled at her—and when they divorced in 1957, Sinatra sold the mansion soon after. It had too many memories, he said.

Now Twin Palms is available to rent as a once-in-a-lifetime experience, and what an experience it is. Okay, so now it's a little less hedonistic and a little more hideaway, but the fabulous architecture alone is worth the price of the night, and of course there are the ghosts that linger on. The house is decorated with many original pieces from this extraordinary era, including Sinatra's original state-of-the-art sound system still in place, although it's not connected for use. There are also the His and Hers change rooms, which blend saucily into the one space (Frank's little joke) and of course there is the cabana and the pool house with bar and kitchenette and the four bedrooms, each with a private ensuite.

None of the house's original furnishings remain, but the current owners have outfitted the place with pieces true to the period, including those designed by Knoll, Vladimir Kagan, T.H. Robsjohn-Gibbings, and Paul Laszlo.

It's clear to see why Sinatra fans and architect followers love Twin Palms. The streamlined design and the way the house hugs the turquoise piano pool entrances all those who wander through the estate. Sinatra wanted the pool to be the centerpiece, the stage for his entertainment and indeed it was—rumor has it Marlene Dietrich and Greta Garbo staged a watery make-out session here one night.

It's also clear to see how Sinatra was inspired here: he launched one of the greatest comebacks in cultural history from Twin Palms, recording his best albums and winning the role in *From Here To Eternity*. If you stand very still in this fabulous house, you can still feel the ghosts of Frank and the Rat Pack swirling around, looking for another drink, playing another joke. It has the feel of being a house well loved, a house well used, and a house that was so beautifully designed even the chink from a champagne bottle tossed during a fight hasn't dented its beauty.

For those who can afford the price, Twin Palms is one of the most extraordinary hideaways in America: a tribute to one of the country's greatest entertainers and a time few will forget.

Photography courtesy Rand Larson

- Architecture/Design: Albert Frey's best
- Highlight: The Movie Colony neighborhood, and the Modernist design
- To pack: Something to read on the lilo, floating around the fabulous pool

MOVIE COLONY HOTEL

Palm Springs, California

Palm Springs first rose to fame in the 1920s when Hollywood stars used to retreat here to escape the watchful eyes of their directors and agents. It became a sanctuary from the movie set, a place where you could forget your scripts, photo shoots, and publicity, refill your martini, and mislay your attire. One of the neighborhoods that the stars gravitated to was the Movie Colony, an enclave of grand mansions tucked away near the centre of Palm Springs. Some of the names who bought homes here included Al Jolson, Barbara Hutton, Cary Grant, Hollywood mogul Darryl Zanuck, Gloria Swanson, Tony Curtis and Janet Leigh, and Jack Benny. Back then you couldn't turn around with spilling alcohol over someone famous.

The stars eventually left or passed away, of course, but the homes remained—remnants of a glamorous, fabulous past. Now, half a century after they hosting the last of their infamous parties, they are being revived by a new generation of architecture lovers and Palm Springs aficionados enamored with the town as much as the myth. Set in the heart of this magnificent colony of properties is the Movie Colony Hotel, an intimate hideaway that perfectly captures the magic of this desert oasis. Full of authenticity and mystery in equal measure, it is one of Palm Springs best secrets: an architectural treasure that allows those captivated with the Movie Colony and its grand past to experience a little of it without having to rent one of the mansions for a movie star price.

Coolly alluring and with a high hip factor, this mostly white boutique hotel is a haven for design lovers—indeed it is one of the hotels responsible for attracting such aesthets to Palm Springs on architectural pilgrimages. The property was designed in 1935 by the Swiss architect Albert Frey, who studied under Le Corbusier in Paris before moving to the US to further his career. He discovered Palm Springs and fell in love with both the desert and the opportunity to create extraordinary mid-century architecture. The Movie Colony was one of Frey's first projects and became a place very dear to his heart long after it was completed.

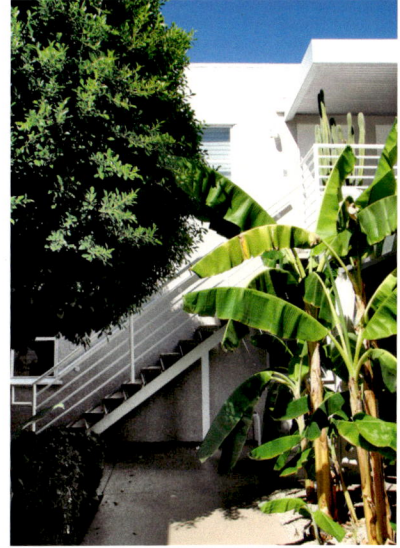

The hotel was originally intended to be a serene, three-townhouse retreat tucked away in the Colony: a place for celebrity houseguests to crash when beds became full in the surrounding mansions, and also as a bolt-hole for stars to come when they needed time away from other stars, or LA in general.

Inspired by the ocean-liner aesthetic, Frey imbued the place with a variety of nautical forms, from the metal railings around the upper decks and terraces to layers of white on the walls. The white was also intended to be a way of both enhancing and offsetting the vast blue desert sky and the ever-present heat. Frey also loved angles—he said that if you want to startle someone, build something at an angle—and the building incorporates many angles that not only suit the streamline architectural style but also provide welcome shade from the intense sun. It is a place full of unexpected planes and curious walkways that lead to fabulous corners, while the cantilevered canopies lend a quiet glamour to the already elegant façade.

For the first few decades of its life, the Movie Colony was a hotel of high style: a place where stars like Jim Morrison of The Doors came, played, and then jumped off balconies into the cool, blue pool. Then, as Palm Springs began to quieten down as a destination, so did the hotel, that is until a group of investors came along, saw the magic, the Frey touches, and the potential in restoring such an iconic gem, and decided to revive it for a new generation of mid-century architecture devotees.

The group, Linda and Walter Haake and interior designer Donald Lloyd Smith, along with the firm of Urrutia Architects, carefully set about bringing the hotel back to life. They stripped back the building to its original bones, restored the suites, the courtyard, and the pool, and then filled the place with pieces from or inspired by the era, including Eames tables, white-leather Wassily chairs, a Nelson marshmallow sofa, 1950s-style silver drinks trays, and an architectural library of mid-century-focused homes.

The highlights include the bar and outdoor living room/kitchen, which doubles as a gathering place and breakfast room, and a glass fire pit with surrounded benches, both of which are quintessentially Palm Springs. But it's the pool that's really captivating: a heavenly slice of turquoise that's the exact same shade as the expansive sky.

The beauty of the Movie Colony Hotel is that it's not overdone, unlike some places in Palm Springs: it doesn't try too hard to please or set out to shock with layers of different architectural styles. It doesn't have to. It was designed by one of the leading modernist architects in North America—a man who always got it right the first time. It is a tribute to mid-century elegance. No wonder it has once again become a much-loved home-away-from-Hollywood for many stars, as well as those with an eye for aesthetics and sophisticated travelers looking for something a little different.

Photography courtesy Janelle McCulloch

- Architecture/Design: Retro inspired
- Highlight: The iconic pool and Oasis garden
- To pack: A good book—you won't be leaving your chaise all day

THE RALEIGH

Miami, Florida

So beautiful it's almost surreal, the regal Raleigh is like no other hotel in Miami. Where other South Beach hotels sit firmly and confidently on the glamorous side of design, encased in acres of sheer, billowy white curtains or featuring dramatic, white-on-white interiors filled with grand statement pieces, The Raleigh has chosen to beat a different design drum. Rather than appearing overtly glamorous and all-too-serious in its study of chic, it has chosen the quieter route. The Raleigh is a study in elegance.

The Raleigh's legendary pool—a sculptural, black-edged, fleur-de-lis masterpiece—is widely regarded as one of the most extraordinary hotel pools in the world, if not the most beautiful pool ever designed period, while the Oasis lounging area, a fabulous black-and-white playground for adults that drifts down to the beach through striped deckchairs, cartoonish change rooms, and fabulously monochromatic daybeds, is just as idolized by the travel and style sets. In fact, the alfresco areas of the hotel are so packed with pretty vignettes and whimsical scenes it's no wonder they're so popular with fashion photographers and production crews looking for dream locations. Even the Raleigh's section of the beach is peppered with stylish black-and-white beach huts and beach shades. It's a photo shoot waiting to happen.

The hotel itself has been around since the 1940s, when the great architect Lawrence Murray Dixon, one of the most acclaimed architects of South Beach's historic Art Deco District, designed it to be one of the showpieces of Miami. As soon as it opened both hotel and pool became instant landmarks, mixing sexiness with elegance in an alluring and compelling vision of beachside grandeur. Esther Williams used it as a backdrop for her films, while Dorothy Parker loved the bold look of The Raleigh so much she decamped here from New York's Algonquin Hotel for some witty repartee in the sun.

When hotelier André Balazs took over in 2002, the building and grounds were certainly in need of some love and care. Balazs, no stranger to grande dame hotels (he had already worked his magic on the iconic Chateau Marmont in LA), set about refurbishing the hotel and bringing it back to its original Art Deco splendor while also injecting his signature style into the corners—that style being one of understatement rather than the flash-and-flesh look preferred by some Miami hoteliers.

Balazs kept the curvaceous lines of the pool and the film star-style glamour of the foyer with its tall, fluted columns, but he added dozens of daybeds and deckchairs, a sprinkling of seductive cabanas, and the Oasis area for guests to lounge about in. He also modernized the rooms, although these aren't as surprising as the public spaces. Finally, Balazs added cute touches such as Raleigh bikes to whiz around town on (black and white naturally), and revamped the 24-hour, retro-style Coffee Bar and Tabac.

There remains a touch of the film-set fabulousness about the hotel but it's now very modern. And while celebrities lounge around the place, the hotel still maintains an air of elegant discretion. In fact, such is its appeal that the Raleigh's 1940s-style Deco charm gets under your skin and wins you over in a way many others can't. Much of Miami can be a little in your face, a little "Hey there, baby," and when all that blatant drama and diva-style becomes too over the top The Raleigh provides the perfect antidote. Take your dark sunglasses, find a daybed, and get ready to relax.

Photography courtesy Nikolas Koenig, Ken Hayden, and Janelle McCulloch

- Architecture/Design: Polished glamour
- Highlight: The front terrace: preen and be seen
- To pack: Something to impress

THE TIDES SOUTH BEACH

Miami, Florida

If you want to hang out with Miami's chic elite, or pretend to be a film star for the day, one of the best places to go is The Tides South Beach. Set in a prime people-watching position on Ocean Drive, facing that sublime stretch of beach, this hotel has recently emerged from a makeover and is still celebrating the new look with a whole lot of hoopla. This is perhaps because the designer responsible for the makeover was none other than Kelly Wearstler, one of America's hottest names in design. Having worked her signature Hollywood Regency look on The Viceroy hotels in Santa Monica and Palm Springs, Wearstler was fully prepared for a new kind of glamour in Miami. And boy, did she get it.

The Tides was the architectural/hotel version of Gloria Swanson in *Sunset Boulevard*—still beautiful in a grand-dame way but requiring a lot of cosseting. Unperturbed, Wearstler set to work. She studied the iconic hotel with its classic 1930s Art Deco design, observed its colorful neighbors, with their near-kitschy, candy-coated hues, and realized the answer to The Tides' refit was retaining a sophisticated aesthetic rather than going all-out on high-wattage glamour. As she says, "I wanted to pay homage to the history of this amazing landmark. My inspiration for the property was 21st-century luxury juxtaposed with casual elegance."

So, taking her cues from the calm palette of the palm trees, boardwalk, and beach opposite, she drenched the lobby, a grand space defined by its enormous scale, in an elegant and innovative mix of stone, cream, gold leaf, and leather, all of which were inspired by either the sea or the textures of the beach, and all of which seem exotic but also welcoming and serene. Then she added lots of oversized lamps and animal-print rugs, swathes of billowy curtains to hide private areas, groupings of 1940s high-backed Senator chairs from Milan, and two distinctive vintage brass palm tree sculptures. It was a bold design move. On the outer terrace, she went for whimsy, with more African touches mixed in with dramatic armchairs. All very unexpected, and all very Wearstler.

When it came to the rooms and suites, however, a different aesthetic was applied; one inspired by sunset colors and vintage recreations. Scattering one-of-a-kind vintage elements in between lots of sunny layers of yellow, Wearstler achieved a retro, yet reassuringly warm effect. Add to this the eye-popping views of the sea and esplanade activity below and you can see why this destination has been an instant hit.

According to Wearstler, the striking décor was designed to honor Miami's beach spirit while respecting The Tides' legendary grandeur. Much of America's media has been in a tizz over the newly refurbished hotel, claiming it has stolen The Delano's design crown and position as "Miami's best hotspot," and Condé Nast *Traveler* magazine voted it among the country's top new hotels for 2008. Even if you're not into glamour, celebrities, or gorgeous design, it is hard not to be impressed by The Tides. Like Gloria Swanson in *Sunset Boulevard*, the old girl has a lot of life in her long legs yet.

Photography courtesy KOR Hotel Group and Janelle McCulloch

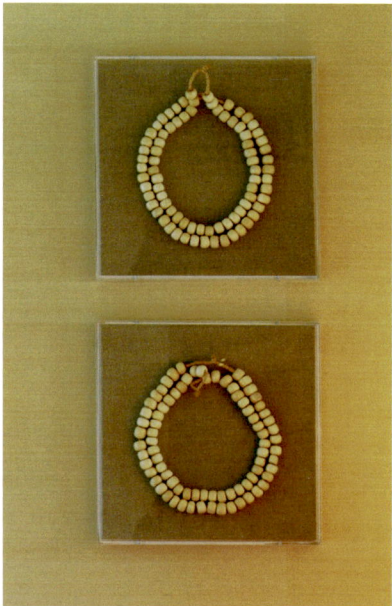

■ Architecture/Design: White-on-white-on-celebrity
■ Highlight: The theatrical foyer
■ To pack: Sexy bikinis—the pool is a buzzing social scene

DELANO HOTEL
Miami, Florida

So much has been written about Delano Hotel that it has become almost as famous as its celebrity guests. Built in 1947 and designed by Robert Swartburg, the landmark hotel has long stood as a beacon in South Beach, its sharp vertical lines, rocket-like fins, and beaming white center tower acting as a kind of architectural lighthouse for beach goers and walkers needing instant coordinates. Then, when Morgans Hotel Group took over in the mid 1990s and commissioned Philippe Starck to redesign the hotel, Delano became a beacon for another reason: it immediately turned into the hottest place in town.

As soon as it re-opened, SoBe partygoers and celebrities-at-rest gravitated to its magnificent white form, oohing and aahing at the glamorous indoor–outdoor lobby, the sophisticated "water saloon", and the theatrical interior. And they haven't stopped coming since. Wandering through Delano one can instantly see the appeal—the design is so dramatic, so spectacular, so surreal that you find yourself wondering if you're in a hotel or a movie set on a back lot in Hollywood.

For a start, there's the grand, gleaming façade with its snappy entrance featuring a deliberately casual outdoor seating area designed almost like a living room with a funky sofa, lampshade chandelier, and contemporary rocking chair. There's the enormous white foyer with its gigantic columns and startling scale. There are the even-more-startling Venetian mirrors and white fur-covered daybeds, plus the quirky statement pieces—wheelbarrow chairs and organically shaped seating juxtaposed with a Gaudi chair, Eames seats, and a series of fabulous high-backed chairs created by Fornasetti. And then there are the swathes of white curtains, like the front of some grand stage where an eagerly awaited Broadway play is about to take place.

The rooms are no less astonishing, having been designed with a mixture of white and surprise. And then there are the outdoor areas, the most captivating of which are the decadent palm tree-lined pool and the garden. The latter is known as The Orchard for its topiary trees with ladders running up them; the former is known as Miami's unofficial daytime nightclub for all the action that takes place there—some outside the cabanas, some inside. Delano is positioned right on the beach, but so much goes on inside the hotel that people not staying here often stand at the beach gate and stare inside, wishing they were guests and not just casual passers-by.

Delano is not for everyone, but it has become popular with the very famous and the very hip. The "water saloon"—which even has a table and chairs in its shallow end, so you can do business or just pose delightfully while keeping your feet cool—is still one of the favored Miami hangouts, a decade after the place opened.

Perhaps the downside to the hype surrounding Delano is that the extraordinary design elements tend to get overlooked. Look closely around the interiors and you'll notice that the design really has some substance. The Brazilian cherry floor, for example, is not only rather grand but lends a serious note to what could easily have been a breezy, almost superficial interior and, along with the paneled walls, gives the hotel the feel of a magnificent library. The museum-style collection of chairs is enthralling to even the non-design-conscious and several spaces, such as the breakfast nook, designed like a cute country kitchen with white marble and timber cupboards, and the dining area, smothered in lots of sexy white leather, stand out as tributes to what is possible in cutting-edge hotel design.

Delano may be facing some stiff competition from other hoteliers eager to upstage it, but this establishment was the first to stand up and show off a new hotel style and it will certainly be flaunting it for a while yet. It's bold, it's brash, and it exudes a cool, charming, and oh-so-sexy attitude. Just like most of its guests.

Photography courtesy Morgans Hotel Group

- Architecture/Design: Miami cool meets Paris elegance
- Highlight: The view from the pool
- To pack: A group of friends—the bar is renowned for its regular parties

HOTEL VICTOR

Miami, Florida

Miami has so many compelling hotels—the cool, the edgy, the classic Art Deco, and the just-plain-glamorous—that the urban environment is almost defined by them. It is a city where you find yourself staring at the buildings as much as the people.

This proliferation of picture-perfect architecture is due in part to the high concentration of well-preserved Art Deco assets and the dedication of conservationists and hoteliers in their restoration and maintenance. By and large, hoteliers have been fairly sensitive in terms of building on glamorous but fragile Art Deco foundations in their endeavors to establish new and refreshed levels of sophistication. Such developers recognize that the secret to the city's lasting success lies in the preservation of Miami's beauty, while creating a happening new scene for those who have never experienced it before.

The Hotel Victor is a prime example of old meeting new in a seamless fusion of traditional and hip. The hotel was originally designed by architect L. Murray Dixon in 1937, but has recently been redesigned by Frenchman Jacques Garcia and is now a little bit Paris, a little bit Miami Beach—although perhaps more Paris than Miami.

Awash with mauves and sea-green shades, the luminous and gracious interior was designed with a compelling nautical theme. Everything from the color palette to the upholstery textures to the enormous jellyfish tank in the foyer subtly references the hotel's proximity to the ocean. Even the whimsical green stools and soft purple banquettes resemble the fluid shapes of delicate sea creatures, while the long, flowing drapes that separate areas and ensure privacy bring to mind the movement of jellyfish in the blue waters of Miami's Biscayne Bay.

Being a Jacques Garcia design though, there is also some French whimsy in the mix: the lime and mauve tones are Parisian-style pretty and similar to the shades often used in French decorating, and the furniture curves in a way that suggests a cheeky Frenchman has been at play here. It's difficult not to imagine that you're in some wondrous, French-directed play about living underwater: the hotel just has that air of stage-show theatrics about it.

The décor was a deliberate move to stand apart from other Miami hotels and hideaways, and The Hotel Victor indeed stands in stark contrast to the next-door Casa Casuarina, Gianna Versace's former mansion-turned-hotel. Best-known for his design work at Paris's famously hip Hôtel Costes, Garcia has an eye for exquisite style and dares to do things other designers may find a little bold. The Turkish Spa has a *hammam* and heated marble slabs, while the bar is an eye-catching space of red and black banquettes that sexily reflect the drinks.

The Hotel Victor also likes to be a little cheeky when it comes to guest services, and in fact made headlines when it appointed a "Vibe Manager," a concierge strictly responsible for the hotel's mood—she'll even choose mood music for your room when she's not organizing the weekly Thursday night parties.

Everything in this hotel has a cheeky side: the restaurants are called Vix (probably for the vixenish vibe) and Vue (no doubt for the people-spotting), while the spa is simply known as "V". Evidently this is not a hotel for retiring types.

The Hotel Victor may be one of the newest kids on Miami's South Beach block, but it's already showing it has the confidence and style to be part of the gang. However, few would have imagined when it was being restored that it would turn out to be this fabulous. Jacques Garcia may have injected a little bit of French fantasy into SoBe after all.

Photography courtesy Janelle McCulloch

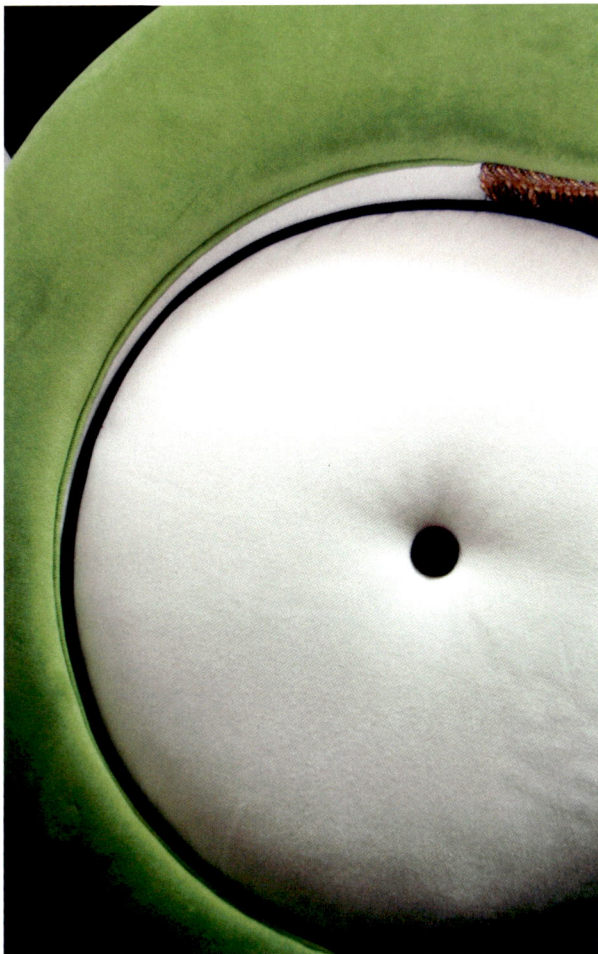

- Architecture/Design: Over-the-top luxury
- Highlight: Everything
- To pack: A swimsuit—the pools are masterpieces of design

THE SETAI
Miami, Florida

Inspired by the 1980s, when everything was bigger, richer, brasher, The Setai is perfectly suited to Miami Beach. It pushes the architectural boundaries out so far you wonder how it gets away with it, but it does and the results speak for themselves. The hotel is magnificent in a jaw-dropping way. And in a town like this, where everything is elaborate and extravagant, that's saying something. It's also unmissable—the 40 stories of aquamarine glass rise up from the beach like a giant gleaming sea creature dominating the landscape. Because of the colour, it tends to blend into the sky, so it's difficult to tell where hotel tower starts and sky ends.

The property actually consists of a residential tower of condominiums and a hotel, both fiercely sophisticated and similar in design. Take the suites, for example. The spas are almost as big as small swimming pools and range in size from 1,300 to 3,500 square feet. The spaces work, however, because the design is pared down so that everything is there for a reason and doesn't infringe or clutter or mess up the lines of sight. The interiors were done by Aman resorts designer Jaya Ibrahim and were inspired by Shanghai's Art Deco period (everything is coolly elegant and in chocolate and honey tones. The atmosphere is subdued and refined and the service impeccably polite).

The contrasting tones are starkly different from Miami's more familiar color scheme of ice cream shades and coral pinks, and the black granite and polished teak can come as a visual shock after you've been on the beach all day, your eyes accustomed to lurid bikinis and brightly painted lifeguard towers. But The Setai's décor is also cool, calming, and easy on the soul, which is often what is needed after a day or a night in Miami. In fact, some guests don't even leave the property: they wander down to the three pools, each heated a slightly different temperature, find a lounge, and lie there in peace all day, among the candle-lit pergolas, cabanas, the courtyard, and sunken seating areas. Why go to the beach when there are delightful poolboys to bring you fresh towels, Evian spray, and water to refresh you on the hour? Why go anywhere again? Unless, of course, you run out of money, which is quite possible here.

The brainchild of architect Jean-Michel Gathy and featuring interiors by Jaya Ibrahim, The Setai is meant to offer a different Miami experience, combining the style of Asia with the fun of the Florida coast. It's very Zen but also very happening. And once you experience the extra accoutrements that come with a $1,150-a-night-room, incuding the Lavazza coffee machine, the Swedish Dux bed, the oversize bath, and the delicious views, you begin to see why this hotel is succeeding.

Photography courtesy Masano Kawana

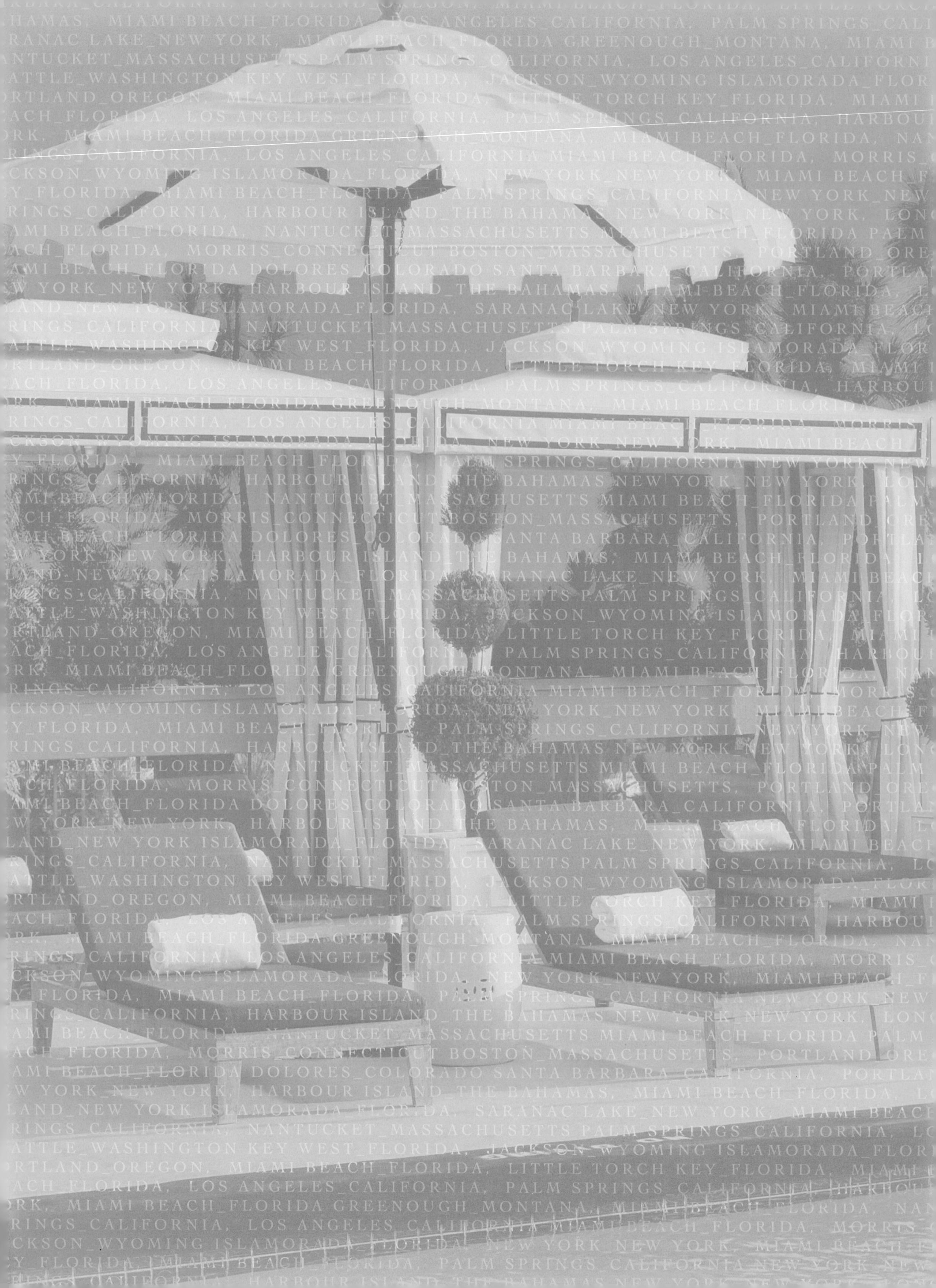

APPENDIX

CONTACT DETAILS

20 **Ace Hotel Portland**
1022 Southwest Stark Street
Portland, Oregon 97205
Phone +1 503 228 2277
acehotel.com

32 **Ace Hotel Seattle**
2423 First Avenue, Belltown
Seattle, Washington 98121
Phone +1 206 448 4721
acehotel.com

188 **Alexander's Guesthouse**
1118 Fleming Street
Key West, Florida 33040
Phone +1 305 294 9919
alexghouse.com

88 **Amangani**
1535 North East Butte Road
Jackson, Wyoming 83001
Phone +1 877 734 7333
         +1 307 734 7333
amangani.com

184 **Casa Morada**
136 Madeira Road
Islamorada, Florida 33036
Phone +1 305 664 0044
casamorada.com

54 **City Club Hotel**
55 West 44th Street
New York, New York 10036
Phone +1 212 921 5500
cityclubhotel.com

226 **Delano Hotel**
1685 Collins Avenue
Miami Beach, Florida 33139
Phone +1 305 672 2000
delano-hotel.com

96 **Dunton Hot Springs**
52068 County Road 38
Dolores, Colorado 81323
Phone +1 970 882 4800
duntonhotsprings.com

108 **El Capitan Canyon**
11560 Calle Real
Santa Barbara, California 93117
Phone +1 866 352 2729
elcapitancanyon.com

26 **Hotel deLuxe**
729 South West 15th Avenue
Portland, Oregon 97205
Phone +1 503 219 2094
hoteldeluxe.com

234 **Hotel Victor**
1144 Ocean Drive
Miami Beach, Florida 33139
Phone +1 305 428 1234
hotelvictorsouthbeach.com

36 **Library Hotel**
299 Madison Avenue
New York, New York 10017
Phone +1 212 983 4500
libraryhotel.com

168 **Little Palm Island**
28500 Overseas Highway
Little Torch Key
Florida 33042
Phone +1 800 343 8567
littlepalmisland.com

174 **Mill House Inn**
31 North Main Street,
East Hampton
Long Island, New York 11937
Phone +1 631 324 9766
millhouseinn.com

140 **Mondrian**
1100 West Avenue
Miami Beach, Florida 33139
Phone +1 305 514 1500
mondrian-miami.com

206 **Movie Colony Hotel**
726 North Indian Canyon Drive
Palm Springs, California 92262
Phone +1 888 953 5700
moviecolonyhotel.com

40 **Night**
132 West 45th Street
New York, New York 10036
Phone +1 212 835 9600
nighthotelny.com

164 **Rock House**
Bay Street, Harbour Island
The Bahamas
Phone +1 242 333 2053
rockhousebahamas.com

82 **The Catalina**
1732 Collins Avenue
Miami Beach, Florida 33139
Phone +1 305 674 1160
catalinahotel.com

74 **The Chamberlain**
1000 Westmount Drive,
West Hollywood
Los Angeles, California 90069
Phone +1 310 657 7400
chamberlainwesthollywood.com

122 **The Crescent**
403 North Crescent Drive
Beverly Hills
Los Angeles, California 90210
Phone +1 310 247 0505
crescentbh.com

ACKNOWLEGMENTS

The Images Publishing Group and Janelle McCulloch would like to acknowledge the following hotels and individuals for their gracious assistance in the production of this book. Particular thanks goes to the following hotels and photographers who supplied additional imagery:

HOTELS

Ace Hotels, Portland and Seattle

Alexander's Guesthouse

Amangani

Casa Morada

City Club Hotel

Dunton Hot Springs

El Capitan Canyon

Hotel deLuxe

Hotel Victor

KOR Hotel Group, for The Chamberlain,
    Viceroy Santa Monica, Viceroy Palm Springs,
    and The Tides South Beach

Little Palm Island

Mill House Inn

Morgans Hotel Group, for Mondrian Miami and Delano

Movie Colony Hotel

Night

Rock House

The Catalina Hotel & Beach Club

The Crescent

The Horizon Hotel

The Landing

The Library

The Mercer

The Moorings

The Point

The Raleigh

The Resort at Paws Up

The Sagamore

The Setai

The Standard Miami

The Veranda House

Townhouse Hotel

Twin Palms

Union Street Inn

Whitelaw Hotel

Winvian

XV Beacon

PHOTOGRAPHERS

Rare Brick

Ken Hayden

Cookie Kinkead

Nikolas Koenig

Eric Laignal

Steven Lam

Rand Larson

Dom Miguel

Sylvia Muller

Miki Ouisterhof

David Phelps